Spring Training

in Sarasota

1924–1960

SPRING TRAINING
IN SARASOTA

1924–1960

NEW YORK GIANTS AND BOSTON RED SOX

JEFF LaHURD

Charleston   London

History
PRESS

Published by The History Press
18 Percy Street
Charleston, SC 29403
866.223.5778
www.historypress.net

Front cover image: Red Sox pitcher Tex Clevenger warms up in front of coach Del Baker in this 1954 photo. Clevenger stayed one year with Boston before moving on to Washington in 1956 and to the New York Yankees in 1961. *Sarasota County History Center*.
Back cover image: Boston Red Sox player. *Sarasota County History Center*.

First published 2006
Manufactured in the United Kingdom
ISBN 1.59629.072.2

Library of Congress Cataloging-in-Publication Data

LaHurd, Jeff.
  Spring training in Sarasota, Florida, 1924-1960 : New York Giants and
Boston Red Sox / Jeff LaHurd.
     p. cm.
  ISBN 1-59629-072-2 (alk. paper)
  1. Spring training (Baseball)--Florida. 2. New York Giants (Baseball
team)--History--20th century. 3. Boston Red Sox (Baseball
team)--History--20th century. I. Title.
  GV875.6.L35 2006
  796.357'640975961--dc22
                              2005033307

Notice: The information in this book is true and complete to the best of our knowledge. It is offered without guarantee on the part of the author or The History Press. The author and The History Press disclaim all liability in connection with the use of this book.

This book is dedicated with heartfelt thanks to Pete Esthus, whose ongoing effort to preserve the images of Sarasota's history is appreciated by all, and to his lovely wife Diane for supporting him in this endeavor.

And to my good friend Nancy Wilkie, who has always been there to help me.

CONTENTS

ACKNOWLEDGEMENTS   9

INTRODUCTION   11

SPRING TRAINING   13

1924–1927   19

1933–1958   49

1959–1960   75

WHATEVER BECAME OF...?   85

BIBLIOGRAPHY   93

ACKNOWLEDGEMENTS

The idea for this book came from an exhibition put on by the Sarasota County History Center on the history of spring training in Sarasota. Some of the research for that program carried over to this book. The exhibition was a success thanks to the hard work of Dave Baber, Ann Shank, Mark Smith, Lorrie Muldowney and Dan Hughes, and I thank them for allowing me the use of some of their material for this publication.

I also want to thank my friend Dick Jackson, who gathered a lot of the material for the exhibition, and thanks also to Ed Lederman for helping me by scanning the images for this book.

As with all of my publications I want to express my gratitude to Pete Esthus for supplying some of the images for this book and for also helping to "accuratize" it for me.

INTRODUCTION

Payne Park was a Norman Rockwell type of a baseball field—small and unsophisticated, a piece of yesterday's Americana where the fans were up close to the players who seemed no farther away than just out of reach.

Of course, such an unpretentious park would not do today. By November 1990, when it was demolished, it was well past its prime. By then, Major League parks, even those in small spring training towns, needed to have a slick, manicured look to them—everything just so—sophisticated, like their larger city counterparts. But from that first spring training season in March of 1924 when the mighty John J. McGraw marched his formidable New York Giants onto the field, until the last Major League ball was pitched there in 1988, this throwback of a baseball diamond, near the heart of downtown Sarasota, hosted the greatest players, managers, coaches and teams that ever trotted on to any field.

If you lived in Sarasota for any length of time, the demolition of Payne Park may have rekindled long forgotten memories of sunny March afternoons, watching from the bleachers as the greats, and the hopeful rookies, prepared for the forthcoming season.

This was assuredly true if you were a little leaguer with a Topps baseball card collection stuffed into a shoebox under your bed, a glove that you treated regularly with saddle soap and a Louisville Slugger propped in a corner of your bedroom.

I was able to watch some of the park's demolition from my office window near the field and recalled a pleasant afternoon sitting in the stands with my grandfather and one of my cousins, my green Citizens Bank little league baseball cap tilted just so, a hot dog in one hand, an RC Cola in the other. The mighty

Yankees were playing the ever-hopeful Red Sox and, while I do not recall who won—although I could guess—the memory of seeing Ted Williams, Mickey Mantle, Whitey Ford, Yogi Berra and the rest of them and of cheering with my grandfather has remained with me for nearly fifty years.

Before the demolition was completed I walked over to the empty field, went into one of the dugouts, stood on the pitcher's mound and remembered the place as it was when I was twelve and with my grandfather. When I left I picked up a piece of a bleacher seat, and brought it home, a souvenir of a sunny March day I'll never forget.

SPRING TRAINING

A young ball player looks on his first spring training as a stage-struck young woman regards the theater.

—*Christy Mathewson, Hall of Fame pitcher*

During the Roaring Twenties, the Florida land boom hit like a bolt of lightning striking a dry pine tree. Instantly the Sunshine State was ablaze and binder-boy salesmen with slick hair, two-toned shoes and plus-four pants fanned the flame of quick riches, and the sparks flew.

Previously, the state had been accessible only to the wealthy who came in the comfort of yachts and private railway cars heading to one of Henry Flagler's or Henry Plant's luxurious resorts. Henry Ford changed all that. His Model T, affordable and durable, along with improved roads, made long-distance travel possible for the masses. Land fever combined with Coolidge prosperity opened the floodgates and in poured hordes of black tin lizzies, with opportunists looking for a chance to make their fortune.

The sentiment, "Build a field and they will come," applied less to the desire to have big-league baseball for its own reward, but rather to attract newcomers to Florida communities striving to grow. Florida was still America's last frontier and only a few cities had any name recognition—Tampa, Miami, St. Petersburg and Jacksonville. The rest were practically unknown and local chambers of commerce realized the gaggle of reporters and photographers who followed the teams could put their towns on the map. For thirty days or so, at the end of each February and through March, daily reports would be wired to New York, Chicago, Philadelphia, Boston, touting the charms of various spring training towns.

Calvin Payne and his wife Martha donated the property for Payne Park in what was described by Karl H. Grismer in *The Story of Sarasota* as "by far and away the most outstanding gift ever made to the city." *Sarasota County History Center.*

Before trekking to the Sunshine State to form the Grapefruit League, Major League teams had been practicing in Texas, Alabama, California and Georgia. A local scribe had no doubts how Sarasota would stack up: "Sarasota is a delightful relief after some of the bald-headed villages in Texas where major league teams trained last season."

Sarasota's field of dreams was named Payne Park, built on a portion of sixty acres of land donated to the city by Calvin Payne and his wife Martha for "park purposes." After accepting the generous gift, Mayor E.J. Bacon declared October 27, 1923, a community workday and the townsfolk came forward—men to do the labor, women to provide refreshments, children to fetch materials. They laid out a baseball diamond, built grandstands, a racetrack and an exhibition building for the county fair. A panoramic picture taken by the Koon's Studio documents their hard work that bright winter day. The photo shows approximately fifty cars, a few trucks, a tractor and a bevy of volunteers going about the task at hand. It's titled: "Building fairgrounds in one day."

The Sarasota Baseball Team had been organized in April of 1912 to "furnish amusement during the summer months and also to advertise the town by having a good baseball team." But with the new construction of Payne Park, Sarastoa set its sights on attracting the big leagues.

Citizens at work on October 27, 1923, laying out a baseball diamond and fair grounds. *Sarasota County History Center.*

The Sarasota Baseball Team's colors were blue-gray with red trimmings and the uniforms arrived in June of 1912, just in time for the game against Bradentown, which they won 8-2. *Sarasota County History Center.*

Sarasota had three false starts attracting Major League baseball to their little field. On February 2, 1922, The *Sarasota Times* announced that if the St. Louis Cardinals came to Bradentown, a Major League team would come to Sarasota. The chamber of commerce was authorized to wire Charles Comiskey of the Chicago White Sox to see if he was interested in bringing his team here. Although Sarasota's connection with Chicago had been very strong since 1910, when internationally renowned Chicagoan Bertha Palmer came here, the deal never materialized.

The next failure-to-appear were Connie Mack's Philadelphia Athletics. The *Times* reported they had been training in Montgomery, Alabama, and selected Sarasota as their next training camp. It didn't happen.

Next to step up to the spring training plate were the New York Yankees, who had been training in Hot Springs, Arkansas. "Babe Ruth and His Team Likely To Be Seen Here," the paper reported. This time the community's chances were enhanced because the city and county had joined to approve a $4,000 expenditure conditional on the citizens raising an additional $6,000 to contract

Sarasota as it looked when the New York Giants first came to town. The land boom would soon transform Sarasota into a thriving community. *Sarasota County History Center.*

The arrival of the New York Giants was welcome news for the community always looking for publicity. *Sarasota Times.*

with a big-league team and bring the field up to professional standards. But the Yankees opted out—strike three.

The *New York Times* reported in November 1923 that Giants manager John McGraw's intimate friend John Ringling had urged him to check Sarasota as a candidate for a spring training site and invited him down during the off season. McGraw, who had ruled out California and San Antonio, said that when he got back from Europe he "was going to take an atlas and make a trip to all the towns that have recommended themselves to us. I want to see what the hotels and ball parks are like and also the climate."

Local fans could be forgiven some skepticism when again it was announced that big-league ball finally was heading to town. The headline on the February 28, 1924 *Sarasota Times* reported, "MCGRAW, WITH REST OF PLAYERS, TO ARRIVE MAR. 1." Indeed, Sarasota had finally hit a home run.

1924–1927

Oh it's great to be young and a Giant.
—*Larry Doyle, New York Giants second baseman*

The juggernaut New York Giants, with firebrand John J. McGraw at the helm, was one of the best teams in the Major Leagues: a powerhouse that had won the World Series in 1921 and 1922, and the National League pennant in 1923. During the Golden Age of Sports, a time when baseball was truly America's favorite pastime, avidly followed throughout the nation, McGraw was one of the most readily known names in the sports world.

John Ringling, with his many New York connections (he was a stockholder in Madison Square Garden, where his circus opened its season each year), was credited with scoring the Giants for Sarasota. The *Sarasota Times* enthused that if the Giants made Sarasota their permanent training home, there should be a monument erected at Five Points with John Ringling on one side and John McGraw (who yielded to the importunities of Mr. Ringling) on the other.

In the midst of Sarasota's anticipation, a few miscues loomed as the Giants began trickling into town. The first group of fifteen players left for Sarasota from New York's Pennsylvania Station on February 21, 1924, aboard the Seaboard Air Line. McGraw, who had been expected to precede the team, hadn't yet arrived. (The paper noted that he was still in Cuba and speculated that, due to Prohibition, it would be quite a long period between drinks, so he determined to remain in Havana.)

The newly arrived sports wags quickly complained that Sarasota's accommodations were completely unsuitable. The Hotel Hunton, "badly

Manager John J. McGraw

The "boss" of the New York Giants, now with his hopefuls at the ball park here. Manager McGraw received a fine welcome from his scores of admirers and friends in Sarasota.

Pen and ink drawing of John McGraw, one of the best baseball managers of all time who ruled his team with an iron fist. *Sarasota Herald.*

rundown," had been reserved, but it could put up only thirty-eight people, and with nine bathrooms was not nearly large enough to house over seventy players plus the mob of reporters. It had been described as a family hotel but the Giants were too large a family. So while Assistant Team Manager Hughie Jennings sought out acceptable rooms, the team spent the day walking the town's streets or sitting on park benches. After several meetings with the building's owner, a deal was struck to put most of the team at the grand and brand new Mira Mar Hotel, which overlooked Sarasota Bay and which, at that time, was expecting only John J. and a few of his coaches. The rest of the team were given rooms at the less glamorous, but acceptable, Watrous Hotel a half block away.

The *New York Times* reported that John Ringling's winter resort was not all that it was cracked up to be and further, he had not prepared the natives for the big-leaguers. This reporter attributed the lodging problem to mixing circuses with baseball: "The circus chief always stays at the fancy hotel while the bareback riders, lion tamers, parachute performers, clowns and circus hands tarry in more modest lodgings elsewhere."

The blame for the debacle was dropped on the doorstep of an unnamed agent of John Ringling's who "owned a winter home and half of Sarasota." He was not in town when the team arrived.

With the lodging dilemma finally resolved—to the relief of the chamber of commerce—the *Sarasota Times* reported, "all of the ear oilers, joy spreaders, crepe hangers and mud slingers are pleasantly [re]located." The paper let it be known that Sarasota was aware of its mistakes and immediately took corrective action. But as to the weather, "we'll consider that out of our jurisdiction, so when the weather don't go off to suit you, just keep your D—— mouth shut."

The problem of where to feed the team also caused a bit of a flap. The Mira Mar Hotel's management had wanted to shunt them off to a small room used by the staff. This too was resolved through a compromise, speedily reached, under which the small room would go back into the exclusive possession of the servants.

An exploratory look at Payne Park drew mixed reviews. While the Giants groundskeeper Henry Fabian said the nicely sodded infield was the best he had seen in any league, the outfield was several inches thick with white sand, "and this horrible discovery brought dismay to General Hughie Jennings and Colonel Cozy Dolan who are in temporary charge of the expedition." They knew McGraw hated sand, which could cause slippery footing, charley horses, wrenched muscles and sore ankles and knees. ("McGraw had struck sand in Gainesville and still swears softly when he thinks of it.") The clubhouse was judged to be top notch, "with room for one hundred and well fitted with lockers, showers, baths, rubbing compartments and even a special room for McGraw painted in blue and cerise."

In summing up the team's first impression of Sarasota, (excepting the "grotesque tangle over hotels") the *New York Times* noted that the town was pleasant, hospitable and pretty; the fishing wonderful and the bathing superb. "On the whole the Giants have no complaints to make about Sarasota."

The team wanted to stage a light practice for Sunday, but because of the Sunday blue laws, were hesitant. The sheriff, however, looked the other way and showed no inclination to send any of the players to the slammer.

On February 26, an all-day downpour helped firm up the outfield but necessitated that training be suspended in favor of the billiard emporium or fishing from the city pier. Two more Giants reported for training that rainy day, Wayland Dean, the "$50,000 pitcher," and catcher Al Stoner. One player departed under mysterious circumstances—Joe Dillard left a note to Jennings saying he was leaving for a reason known only to him, and bought a train ticket to Atlanta.

THE BAT FOR THE SLUGGER

A bat just right in length, weight and grasp. A bat that will co-operate with you in knocking the old pill high, wide and handsome.

You will also find besides trusty bats a complete line of SPAULDINGS QUALITY BASEBALL EQUIPMENT AT THIS STORE.

Whatever equipment you may need—let GARDNER - NOBLE SERVE YOU.

GARDNER-NOBLE
Palm Ave., Mira Mar Block

The Sarasota County
Board of County Commissioners
Again Welcome

THE NEW YORK GIANTS

Louis Lancaster, Chairman

COMMISSIONERS

J. Paul Gaines	F. Ziegler
J. J. Crowley	Guy Reagan

A HOME RUN

"Gets You More Than A Three Base Hit—Even During The Training Season,"

All Ball Players Are Welcome And Will Unknowns—Patronize William Dorflinger At The Mira Mar Barber Shops.

(Late of Bankers Club, N. Y.)

A'l Ball Players Are Welcome And Will Get First Class Service

Get your feet in good working order.

DR. LOBB

Graduate Chiropodist and Orthopedist is located in the Mira Mar Barber Shop.

Above and left: A welcoming greeting from the Sarasota County Commission and some advertising for the players. *Sarasota Times.*

Without iron-fisted McGraw in town to lord over his hot-blooded players, there had been some unwanted fraternization with the townies. When he finally arrived on March 2, he set their schedule: in bed by eleven, up at eight for a hard day's workout. The *Sarasota Times* wondered if "maybe now some of the dames will get a little rest, 'cause this bunch of Giants is the shiekinness bunch of Giants that ever wandered our way. [They] have captured the hearts of the few maidens in our midst." McGraw would not have been surprised at the goings-on. He had once said, "One percent of baseball players are leaders of men. The other ninety-nine percent are followers of women."

Unfortunately, the wooing of local damsels by out-of-town athletes brought forth the wrath of the ever-vigilant Ku Klux Klan. The paper opined that it was not unlikely that the Ku Klux Klan parade "was sponsored by reason of complaints pitifully carried to them by some heretofore considered local sheik. Handbills announced the Klan was marching on the orders of the Great Titan, Province Four of the Realm of Florida, noted the route and ended with, We were here yesterday; we are here today and by the Grace of God we will be here tomorrow."

On a Thursday evening, approximately one hundred white-hooded "men of mystery" formed up north of town on Central Avenue and marched, in a column of twos, toward Main Street. Led by a lone horseman, they carried the Stars and Stripes "and an array of streamers, standards and principles upon which the Klan is supposed to be founded, which created considerable comment among both men and women." By the time the protectors of Sarasota's feminine virtue arrived at Five Points it was 8:30 and fifteen hundred men, women and children had gathered—"a moving mass of people." The Giants' impression of this self-righteous display of indignation is not known, but it was a dubious welcome to Sarasota, the City of Glorified Opportunity.

Within a few days, mutual misgivings were soon put aside as the team, the town and the reporters settled into a comfortable relationship, each fulfilling their responsibilities: the Giants working hard to prepare for the coming season and providing spirited ball playing for the fans, the townsfolk supporting the team and the scribes sending stories of Sarasota's abundant virtues northward.

Fiery McGraw, called the most notable character in balldom, made for good copy. He had started in the big leagues with the Baltimore Orioles of the National League when he was seventeen—a rough player turned tough manager. In its early days, baseball was often a rugged, no-holds-barred sport and no one personified that side of the game more than John J. McGraw. His sometimes explosive coaching style could be compared to that of Woody Hays, Bobby Knight or Billy Martin. McGraw once said, "With my team I am absolute czar. My men know it. I order plays and they obey. If they don't, I fire them." He was called "Little Napoleon." When one of his players questioned him, McGraw berated, "Don't ever talk to me. I speak to you and you just shut up." He was comfortable yelling at umpires, managers, other players and his own team members. But he was a winner at baseball, and to him, that's all that mattered.

His method of coaching was summed up: "Sportsmanship and easygoing methods are all right, but it's the prospect of a fight that brings out the crowds." He knew how to fill the Polo Grounds, the Giants' home stadium. In 1924, 844,068 fans came to watch McGraw's brand of baseball. (He also knew how to fight. In 1920 he was expelled from the Lambs Club in New York for what amounted to a brawl with fists and chairs a-flying, though two men—Wilton Lackaye and John C. Slavin—ended up in the hospital.)

A season ticket in 1924 went for $11.00 for grandstand seats or $5.50 for a seat on the bleachers. Initially, there were only six home games scheduled, but more were promised and workouts could be watched. But there was worry that tickets weren't selling quickly enough. The guarantee that brought McGraw's team to town had not been deposited and the newspaper worried of the impending disaster if ticket sales did not pick up.

The day after his arrival, McGraw banned his players from playing golf—not a popular move, but McGraw was not much on popularity contests. Previously, he had tolerated the Scottish sport, but like several other Major League managers he wanted his players to be thinking *only* of baseball, not contemplating how to improve their golf game. In deigning to explain his motives McGraw said, "Golf is a great game and I'm for it, but like everything good, it can be overdone. In fact, golf is too good, for it sometimes grips a ball player so tightly that he gives more attention to perfecting his midiron shots than he does to polishing off his batting style." Ty Cobb, at the time the manager of the Detroit Tigers, had also barred golf, and while several members of the team were upset by the decision, golf would remain for the Giants fine in the wintertime but not in the baseball season. All thoughts and activities had to be focused on winning the pennant.

During his first week in town, McGraw delivered a message to the local Kiwanis Club, many of whose members were the movers and shakers of Sarasota, telling them that if hotel accommodations could be found for his team, the Giants would come back in 1925 and possibly for years to come. "Give me good weather, a good ball park and adequate hotel facilities and I will be satisfied." The club was told that McGraw had written to Giants President

Mighty Babe Ruth, the Sultan of Swat (second from right), with friends on the links at the Bobby Jones Municipal Golf Course.

Taking a swat. According to the United States Golf Association website, Ruth and Ty Cobb were involved in a golf rivalry. Cobb won the "Ruth" cup by besting the Babe in the best of three matches. Cobb proudly displayed the cup on the mantle above his fireplace, next to his Baseball Hall of Fame plaque. *Sarasota County History Center.*

Charles A. Stoneham telling him that in all his twenty-odd years, McGraw had never seen a finer training camp than Sarasota.

On March 6, the Giants had a well-attended tune-up game with the University of Florida. McGraw used two of his big guns to pitch: rookies Wayland Dean and Ernest Maun. They slaughtered the collegians 17 to zip. Hardly a surprise, as the Giants had five future Hall of Fame players on the 1924 roster: Frankie Frisch, Ross Youngs, George Kelly, Bill Terry and Fred Lindstrom.

McGraw gave the team a day off on March 9 and answered press questions about the rumor that he might consider retiring in the next couple of years—fat chance! He quashed the sacrilege, saying that he was not contemplating seriously any move to quit as an active manager. He was just as enthusiastic about the 1924 squad as he had been in 1903 and 1904. "Some people are fond of saying that the day I quit as manager of the Giants will be the one day when I'm so old and feeble that they can't drag me from the bed to the ball park. Well, that is not true. I'll step down long before that time."

An inter-squad game between the "Yannigans" (early twentieth-century baseball term signifying a rookie) and the regulars again saw impressive pitching by Dean and Maun, with the Yannigans besting the regulars 4–0. McGraw was trying to get as much work in as he could in preparation for the game against the St. Louis Cardinals managed by Branch Rickey.

This first game of the 1924 spring season, opened on March 15 "with appropriate pomp and ceremony." On hand was the Sarasota Municipal Band, smartly uniformed and led by Merle Evans, playing "everything except 'The Star Spangled Banner.'" (It was not explained why, of all songs, "The Star Spangled Banner" was not played.) The guest of honor, on hand to toss out the first ball, was John Arnold Heydler, the National League president. The *Times* noted that he was nattily attired in a stunning sartorial combination of white duck trousers, blue coat and straw hat.

Nearby Bradenton was the training town for the Cards, and a small but noisy contingent had come to watch the game. As each player took his turn at bat he was given an ovation by the excited spectators, thrilled that Major League baseball had arrived in Sarasota.

The Giants went on to a 6–4 win, "eminently satisfactory to the loyal citizens who came out and rooted for the home boys with might and main." McGraw too was pleased. He gave the team the next day off and even lifted his golfing ban for that sunny Sunday. While some of the players took to the links, others went to Crescent Beach to swim and others fished or went boating.

By the March 20 game with the White Sox, the stadium was filled to capacity as the Giants nipped the Sox in a game that went twelve innings and was described as one of the best baseball games that had ever been played on Florida soil. One of the Giants' stars that day, Ross Youngs, a favorite of McGraw's because of his hustle, contracted Bright's disease, a kidney disorder, and died in 1927 at age thirty.

Although the Giants would continue playing exhibition games on their way to New York, Sarasota's last spring training game in 1924 was on March 29. The *Sarasota Times* had noted the initial problems between the community and the Giants, but when the team left they were sent off as "best of friends." A few days later a headline announced: "M'GRAW WILL BRING N.Y. GIANTS BACK TO SARASOTA IN SPRING OF THE NEXT SEASON."

The consensus was that the Giants had put Sarasota on the map and the town had gotten "more advertising in the last sixty days than in any similar period of its history." The *Sarasota Times* wanted the team back, noting that while some early reports sent by out-of-town scribes were critical because of the problems with accommodations, it was not the team's fault what reporters wrote. McGraw had been a consistent booster. As for the players, the paper told readers that the ball players would be found less noisy, better behaved and less quarrelsome than the native young men of the town in which they spend the early spring.

The Giants went on to a 93–60 season in 1924; good enough to win the National League pennant, but they lost the World Series to the Washington Senators 4 games to 3. They might have taken the series, but outfielder Jimmy O'Connell (who had cost the Giants $75,000, the highest price ever paid for a minor leaguer) and coach Cozy Dolan (hired in 1920) had been put on the ineligible list for trying to bribe Philadelphia Phillies shortstop Heinie Sand to "not bear down too hard" on them during the last game in the fight for the pennant. The two players were banned forever from baseball by the no-nonsense Commissioner Judge Kenesaw Mountain Landis, who had been hired in 1920 by team owners after the Black Sox scandal and given carte blanche to clean the sport up. Sportswriter Heywood Broun described Landis this way: "His career typifies the heights to which dramatic talent may carry a man in America if only he has the foresight not to go on the stage."

A bright spot that year for McGraw was his reinstatement into the Lambs Club. Three hundred signed the petition to allow him back with the news release noting that the "encounters which sent Wilton Lackaye and John C. Slavin to the hospital are recalled."

I think we can win if my brain holds out.
—John McGraw

When the Giants players—"the shipment of possible pennant material"—began returning for spring training in February of 1925, Sarasota was a dramatically changed town and, indeed, was on the map. The population had nearly doubled and the reporter accompanying the team wrote that they scarcely recognized the place. The city's missteps of the previous year had been replaced with clockwork precision and accommodations were roomy and comfortable in the new Hotel Sarasota. Even the weather was better with an arrival temperature of eighty-two, cooled by a bay breeze and not a cloud in the sky.

Along with the rest of Florida, Sarasota was booming as the great land fever took hold. One resident recalled that the city was electric with excitement, while another remembered that the cash registers were singing. Sarasota was charged up and full of itself. (One of the traveling scribes remarked that baseball had made Sarasota. As he put it, "baseball was the Prince Charming that came along and kissed Princess Sarasota awake…Thousands of words nightly from a town that nobody had ever heard of before.")

Everywhere one looked, building projects were going full steam as the area began to be filled in with hotels, banks, schools, churches, restaurants, theatres, subdivisions, palatial homes and all the other amenities of a desirable town. The *Sarasota County Times* described "transaction after transaction of great magnitude follow[ing] closely one another with amazing rapidity." On hand at the train station were fast-talking real estate salesmen making their pitches, while jazz music blared from real estate offices downtown.

Nowhere was the spirit of the new Sarasota more obvious than in the advertisements showcasing new housing developments, some of them bona fide, others only lines on a plat map. Some parcels of property—or rather a binder on a parcel—sold several times in the morning and several times in the afternoon at ever-escalating prices and were never recorded. The purpose was less to buy a homesite on which to build than to make some bucks in turning it over to someone else at a higher price. Typical of the hype was an advertisement for Longboat Shores being promoted by A.S. Skinner: "You Can't Fail to Make Big PROFITS If you Invest Now In Longboat Shores." C.L. Richardson was selling FAIRWAY by assuring "Today's Decisions MEAN Tomorrow's Profits."

Mighty John McGraw, never averse to making a few bucks, be it in baseball or real estate, got caught up in what seemed like easy money. By the end of 1925, he had lent his name and reputation (now polished to a bright sheen) to one

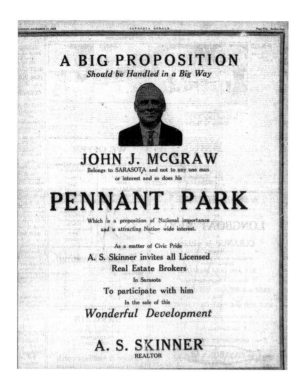

Above and right: John J. McGraw got caught up in Sarasota real estate, but his Pennant Park development failed, prompting McGraw to take his Giants team elsewhere for spring training after the 1927 season. *Sarasota Herald.*

of the most heavily advertised projects of the era—Pennant Park Subdivision, "One of the Most Beautiful Bits of Homeland in the World."

Located on Sarasota Bay just north of Whitfield Estates, homesites at Pennant Park were offered for $2,500 to $10,000 with as little as $625 down. The streets were to be named after baseball stars of the day, with the main thoroughfare called Mathewson Avenue to honor "the greatest pitcher of all time," and one of McGraw's favorite players, Christy Mathewson, who died at age forty-five of TB in October of 1925. Two artists from New York offered to erect a statue at no charge of the great man at the entranceway to the neighborhood.

A New York syndicate spent ten days scouting the property in February of 1926 and pronounced it perfect as a hotel site. The *Sarasota Herald* reported that Pennant Park could have a hotel any time it wanted if John J. McGraw accepted the proposition of the syndicate.

McGraw, who had been a roughhouse player during the league's less refined days and a firebrand manager whose antics were well reported up north, was portrayed locally as a gentleman of sterling character—the "Roosevelt of Sport—Clean, Honorable, Trustworthy—A Winner." Winner was the only unarguable word.

One advertisement solemnly proclaimed, "There isn't a man who has ever been admitted to John J. McGraw's friendship who wouldn't walk across the brimstone pit on a rotten rail to serve him." His abrasive personality traits were not conducive to salesmanship.

McGraw's astute gamesmanship was said to also apply to investing in real estate. "Watch That Man On Third!" blared one of the ads. "That's the advice that I John J. McGraw have given a thousand times to my team...THE MAN ON THIRD, the man who is going to steal a run on you is the man who has already sent in his check for a reservation for a home-site in PENNANT PARK." A coupon was printed on the page to snip and send in with a check, lest the man on third steal your homesite. Another ad, showing a stiffly smiling McGraw warned, "You're striking out every day. Unless you have already clipped and sent in the coupon...with a check for $200 pinned to it. The minute you do that, you line out a homer." A full-page ad in the January 17, 1926 edition of the *New York Times* with an inset picture of McGraw in a suit and hat promised, "I Am Building Another Winner in Which YOU May Share."

On December 18, 1925, the banner headline for the *Sarasota Daily Times* announced "395 ACRES, COST $987,500, ADDED TO PENNANT PARK." That brought the development's size up to 1,451 acres, "one of the best and biggest developments in the state." The development was said to have five thousand lots and was advertised throughout the country with real estate offices in the major cities.

McGraw with some real estate executives about to take off for a birds-eye view of Sarasota and his property at Pennant Park, on Sarasota Bay, just north of Whitfield Estates.

The list of Sarasotans who bought home sites in Pennant Park included many of the town's movers and shakers: J.H. Lord, A.B. Edwards, C.N. Payne (who had donated the grounds for Payne Park), Ralph C. Caples, Charles Ringling and numerous others. The mayors of Bradenton and Palmetto were said to be among the buyers. As it was situated between Sarasota and Bradenton, the development was hawked there as well and according to the paper, "the people of Bradenton have taken to Pennant Park like a parrot to sunflower seeds." McGraw began to be cited in the *Sarasota Herald* as "the well known realtor," and "realtor and sportsman."

After the hurricane of September 1926, which hit Miami with such dramatic force, the boom began to peter out. For places like Pennant Park the party was over. By the end of that year the deleterious effects of the bust were being felt throughout the community. The ranks of fast-talking salesmen dried up and instead of glowing accounts of Sarasota's rosy future, the local news was of mortgage foreclosures, bankruptcies, suits and counter suits. According to Karl Grismer in his *Story of Sarasota*, "[McGraw] spent no money on developments but even so, his salesmen sold about $100,000 worth of lots."

The first of the players, the pitchers and catchers, left a chilly New York on February 21, 1925, aboard the Seaboard Airline Railway. That year the roster was down to thirty-seven men, including eighteen pitchers, five catchers, seven infielders and seven outfielders. McGraw assured fans that what the Giants lacked in quantity they more than made up for in quality. As the train headed south to sunny Sarasota it stopped for players in Philadelphia, Baltimore and Washington, finally arriving in town before noon. They were on the field and in uniform for drills at two that afternoon.

After a mild workout many of the players changed into their plus-fours, gathered their golf clubs and headed for the links, just across the street from Payne Park. Some of the players spent the afternoon sightseeing. These leisurely pursuits would change when Little Napoleon rolled into town. Of the first workout, a *New York Times* reporter wrote, "Candor forces the admission that today's workout did not amount to much. Everyone was in uniform and everybody had his picture taken and ran once about the park and that was about all there was to it."

The weather was beautiful, and the next day's practice was equally brief. For the first time in the team's history there was only one practice session consisting of an hour warm-up and one lap around the park. A reporter who accompanied McGraw and the team for twenty years said that it was the first time in memory that the Giants "had not done two hitches a day, and hard ones at that." He noted that "the sojourn of the National League champions on the shores of Sarasota Bay will not be a time for golf, fishing, swimming and idle hours [as] Mr. McGraw will be here tomorrow and the Giants will be ready for the opening of the season in April. They always have been."

A rumor soon circulated that John Ringling was going to buy a controlling interest in the club. It was said that he and a group of investors were interested in purchasing the stock of Charles A. Stoneham, the club's majority owner. McGraw, in this plan, would continue as manager and minor stockholder. When he arrived in Sarasota from a cruise with Ringling to Cuba aboard Ringling's yacht *Zalophus*, McGraw would neither confirm nor deny. He told reporters, "I have absolutely nothing to say one way or the other." Ringling could not immediately be reached for comment. A few days later, McGraw announced: "The report that Charles A. Stoneham is about to sell the New York Giants to a syndicate headed by John Ringling and Colonel T.L. Huston is absolutely without foundation."

The first session under McGraw was brisk. The paper noted, "The hitting was cleaner and harder and the fielding sharper. The pitchers, of course, were still taking things easy." Pitcher Arthur Nehf, a left-hander from Terra Haute, was said to be so overweight that "his nickname, Lil Arthur, fits him badly." He worked hard, in spite of a bad cold, to get down to playing trim. Bill Ryan, another pitcher, was also said to be overweight. "Ryan is another that can spare some poundage and will probably have to when McGraw takes hold."

Interestingly, the scribe from New York said the community seemed not to show much interest in the club. "There have not been ten spectators to watch the Giants in four days. The inhabitants know that there are some strangers in town, but they think they are real estate men. Not even the schoolboys seem to have the slightest interest in baseball."

There were a few holdouts for McGraw to contend with as he started shaping his team that spring, but one by one most of them fell into line as their issues were resolved. The team captain, Frank Frisch—the Fordham Flash—was conspicuously slow to sign on the dotted line. Frisch was said to be aloof from McGraw, while McGraw was said to be displeased. Before he had journeyed south, the unsigned captain didn't anticipate any trouble with his contract. He reportedly thought a short conversation with McGraw would settle the matter. He was wrong.

At the suggestion of an unyielding McGraw, Frisch went to majority owner Stoneham to plead his case for an increase in his salary to $25,000. Frisch thought he was worth as much as Rogers Hornsby of the Cardinals who had signed a three-year contract for $100,000. Frisch finally signed for his old salary, but with another delay, as he was on the links. Team Secretary Jim Tierney explained that "the sturdy son of Fordham had a previous engagement in the shape of a golf foursome and, of course, such a trifling affair as a $20,000-a-year contract could not be expected to keep a true golfer from the links." (In recapping Frisch's salary with the Giants organization, which he joined in 1919, the *New York Times* reported without comment that he had received about $60,000 in salary and another $20,000 from the four World Series he played in thus far.)

A young Texas pitcher, "Dangerous Dan McGrew," who had three undistinguished years with Washington, went missing at contract-signing time. "Both Messrs. McGraw and Ringling are anxious. If he fails to make good as a pitcher, Ringling is prepared to offer him a contract." At 6' 6" and 235 pounds, the towering pitcher was said be too big to hide in Sarasota. Young Walter McGrew, "the towering terror of Yoakum, Texas" who was dissatisfied with his salary, was ultimately found, talked to and sent packing to the Memphis club "with thanks." (McGrew was likened to a promising infielder named Fuller who had been offered two contracts and rejected them both. McGraw sent him back and "that was the last that was ever heard from Mr. Fuller in the exclusive circles of the major leagues.")

Other holdouts seeking increases included Emil Meusel and Bill Terry—the "California Clouter" and the "Memphis Mauler"—which pleased McGraw not at all. He thought it unfair to the other players. "If a man comes down here to do his best and makes good the Giants will meet him half way," said McGraw. "But I am here to train my ball club and not dicker with dissatisfied players over their salary." (Of Terry, McGraw was quoted that "he could ask for more money in winter and do less in summer than any other ball player I know.")

On March 2, McGraw, in uniform and on the field, put the team through a double session workout. It was reported that he was hitting and fielding with the best of them but did not show much speed on the bases. Frisch still had not signed, but McGraw seemed to be more worried about absent first baseman George "High-pockets" Kelly who had not been heard of since the fall. But, the local paper pointed out, "it is Long George's usual custom to drop into camp unannounced." And drop in he did.

After two inter-squad games between the rookies and regulars with each group winning one, McGraw chose nineteen players, including four rookies who showed promise, to take the trip to Palm Beach for two games with the champion Washington Senators. He gave the rest of the team a holiday.

The Giants triumphed over the Senators, rallying late in both games, and came back to Sarasota with McGraw so pleased with the team's performance that he ordered a light workout on March 12 as a reward. By then Terry and Meusel had signed, leaving only two others, catcher Snyder and Kelly without signed contracts.

On the fourteenth, the Giants beat the Phillies 4–1 in Sarasota in a game that saw Phillies manager Arthur Fletcher banished from the game in the eighth inning for heatedly questioning a called third strike by umpire Walker who told him that there would be no more baseball until he left the field.

A week later, having several more games under his belt, McGraw made the necessary cuts. Of the rookies, only outfielder Frank Walker, catcher Mickey Devine and pitcher John Wisner were retained. Tabs would be kept on the others but the paper assured that they "would not be seen around the Polo Grounds this summer."

The Giants had to face the Phillies again, and play the St. Louis Browns and Boston Braves before they began their journey home, playing more teams along the way. In Jacksonville, The Gate City, they had another match with the Senators and McGraw declared his Giants were in shape for the forthcoming campaign. The only negative that McGraw mentioned was that holdout Frisch had injured his arm while swimming at Sarasota Beach. "We had a good training camp—only Frisch's accident has marred it—a lot of fine weather, and the result is that I have my team pretty well along." During the

1925 regular season the Giants went 86–66, good enough for second place in the National League.

Learn to know every man under you, get under his skin, know his faults. Then cater to him—with kindness or roughness as his case may demand.
—*John McGraw*

At the start of the 1926 season, an interesting twist was added to the often already tenuous contract negotiations. Emboldened by the same big buck bug that bit McGraw, some players took a page out of his financial playbook and looked to real estate sales as a fallback in the event that they could not cut a deal with Little Napoleon. At the beginning of 1926, people were still making oodles of fast, easy money in land speculation. By the end of the year, that would change dramatically.

Harry Cross, traveling with the team for the *New York Times*, reported that Mart Kuppish had come up from Miami to try to get a spot on the Giants roster but wasn't worried about it from a financial standpoint because he could "go right back into the real estate business where he admits he can hit over .400 anytime." The realtors, Cross wrote, wanted native son Kuppish to make it in the bigs to keep the memory of the state warm in the minds of the baseball public.

Cross also reported that for a time, baseball was second fiddle to the development of Pennant Park; that McGraw was devoting the first week in February only to Pennant Park, and had been going between New York and Sarasota all winter "to transform some of the jungles along Sarasota Bay into a fair garden spot. His mind has been full of ideas of titles and deeds, of boulevards and terraces." Cross noted that the sidewalks were "jammed with realtors…doing business on the curb market…willing and ready to swap one partly submerged lot for two above water, at any time or any place."

Holdout Jack Scott, whose whereabouts had been unknown to the team, surfaced in "a suburb with the pretentious name of Venice," saying that he was doing so well in real estate he would not sign a contract "unless there is a change made in the arithmetical features." The pitcher had come to camp on his own dime, "looking fit as a fiddle" but "in something of a belligerent mood." He wanted a raise in salary or he was going back to his home—presumably after he made a killing in real estate—to hunt and fish. Scott told reporter Cross that he paid his own way down and he could pay his own way back if McGraw didn't give him satisfaction. McGraw, whose negotiating style could be characterized as "my way, or the highway," confessed to being not that impressed with Scott's performance during the previous season where he went 14–13 and "fell down during the hot weather." McGraw recommended against a raise and told the pitcher he could sign the contract or hop back on the train. McGraw let it be known that he had a slew of pitchers and he was willing to give some of the new talent a try. Scott left on a northbound. Said Cross: "He was shooting for a high salary, but his marksmanship was bad." (Real estate and hunting and fishing notwithstanding, Scott later signed and went 13–15 during the 1926 season.)

The team took up lodging at Charles Ringling's Sarasota Terrace Hotel, adjacent to the ball field and the golf course. The hotel was still under construction, surrounded by scaffolding and building equipment but the players were given rooms on the completed sixth and seventh floors. Cross noted as the team arrived, "Sunshine floods the countryside and the first things the ball players looked for were straw hats and flannel togs."

Interestingly, Cozy Dolan, who had been banished from baseball after the 1924 season, turned up in Sarasota promoting the local greyhound track. According to the *Sarasota Herald*, he had been in town a couple months before the team began arriving and had made plenty of friends. In an article about his banishment from the game, his friends speculated that, always a kidder, he had tried to play a joke on the naïve Jimmy O'Connell but that it backfired badly. "He probably told the verdant lad a lot and thought he was kidding the lad, but the kidding backfired—O'Connell, as recruits are often wont to do, took it seriously." There was hope that Landis would relent and reinstate both men. The paper felt Landis made an Alp out of a Florida ridge.

Co-manager Jennings had taken sick and could not come immediately down, so this year McGraw was on hand when the first arrivals got off the train in downtown Sarasota. The team immediately got into their uniforms and on to Payne Park field to begin the process of getting into shape.

Jennings was replaced with Roger Bresnahan, "The Duke of Tralee," who had broken into the big leagues with the Washington Senators at age eighteen. Over a seventeen-season career, six with the Giants (1903–1908), Bresnahan was said to be able to play every position, and play it well. He studied at the McGraw school of baseball and in his younger days was known as a scrapper— in fact "an unabashed Irish brawler," who was often fined, ejected from games and suspended. Having played every position in baseball, he was expected to be a big help to McGraw.

To the relief of many who worried that McGraw was devoting too much time and energy into Pennant Park at the cost of his team, it was announced in

This Is to Inform You That Bresnahan Is a Happy Giant

HE CAME TO THE U.S. WHEN A LAD

HOW DO THEY MISS 'EM?

ROGER BRESNAHAN

HE STARTED OUT AS A PITCHER

IN 1902 HE CAST ASIDE THE FINGER MITT FOR THE BIG ONE.

© CENTRAL PRESS ASSN.

Roger Bresnahan, 'The Duke of Tralee,' brought down to help McGraw with management duties, could play every position well. He was inducted into the Hall of Fame in 1945. *Sarasota Herald.*

the *Sarasota Herald* on February 26 that he had put his affairs in the hands of a trust company and "that he would give his undivided attention to coaxing the Giants to another pennant."

But when Bresnahan was featured in an article two weeks later, the paper reported that McGraw would depend mightily on his old friend because "McGraw's real estate interests here take much of his time. He tries to visit the ball park daily but finds little time to oversee details of the training." It would be left to the well-rounded Bresnahan to take charge of the squad when McGraw was otherwise occupied.

Two new players quickly caught McGraw's eye: a seventeen-year-old, just out of high school named Melvin Ott, and Fay Thomas, "a huge boy from the University of Southern California [who] looks as if he could throw a ball fast enough to go through a brick wall." According to McGraw, Ott was "as rare a baseball possibility at the age of seventeen as his experienced eyes ever rested upon, while Fay [had] in his possession the greatest fastball in camp." In describing Ott's play during a workout the *Herald* wrote that "he found one of [pitcher] Ring's slants to his liking in the fifth and sent [outfielder] Young to the tall weeds in deep right to look for it. The Giant fly chaser had some trouble in distinguishing the pill from the various assortment of tropical growth he encountered on his jungle exploration and the time consumed proved sufficient to let the Yannigan catcher circle the bases."

Pitcher Jimmy Ring had signed on with the Giants with the hope that his past performances against the Pirates would "make the Pirates quake in their shoes." Ring cared not at all about the new rule allowing pitchers to use resin bags, which some thought would give pitchers new advantages. "All this talk about the resin bag bringing back trick pitching is simply hysterical talk. It will help the curve ball tossers, but there is no danger that it will bring back the 'sailor,' the 'floater' or any of the other weird deliveries which caused so much consternation to the batters."

Ring may not have worried about the resin bag, but his arrival weight of 190 pounds motivated him to work early and hard to get into shape. It was prophesized that "in a few days he will not be such a burden on the clubhouse scales."

Workouts started on February 22 and for the first couple days were limited to one session per day. After the players limbered up and took to the warmer climate they would "cut loose and get in shape for the exhibition games and then to the more strenuous occupation of annexing a pennant." The field was in great shape, taken in hand by Henry Fabian, "the landscape gardener of Harlem who smoothed out the lawn."

During their free time the players had an array of recreational activities to occupy them. There were a couple movie theatres in town, a billiard hall, two free concerts a day, dances at the Mira Mar Auditorium, the dog track and of course the beaches. McGraw got a group of men together for a fishing trip in the Gulf of Mexico, a trip some joked had been "organized by the Giants' pilot solely for the purpose of getting some landlubbers sick."

Many players were still unsigned, having been given a sense of independence by the money they could make selling in the fast-paced real estate market. As Cross stated, "If Manager McGraw has learned the value of arguing in his new business Pennant Park, so have the players and the coming week will probably see more combative talking, pro and con between ball players…than in any previous season." Virgil "Zeke" Barnes, however, signed as soon as he got off the train from Kansas, taking to heart McGraw's assertion that he could wait in Kansas until a pail of water freezes in a Pittsburgh blast furnace before his demands would be met. Barnes wisely felt it prudent to get to Sarasota as quickly as possible and "get his fountain pen into action." (After Barnes held out in 1923 and 1924, it was said that he seemed to be getting in the habit McGraw was going to help him break it.) Of the other holdouts, McGraw said that they needed the money more than he needed their services.

By March 5 the squad was in good enough shape for a hard-fought practice game that was characterized by "hard hitting, circus catches in the outfield and some snappy play by the inner works." The weather had been accommodating and it was felt that the team was much further along than during previous spring training years.

McGraw had seen enough to be able to make the first cuts and the next day he put two players on the train to the Little Rock team of the Southern League.

The first bona fide game of the regular spring season saw the guys from Gotham beat up on the University of Florida Gators by the lopsided 11–3 in front of a small group of fans. By the end of the fifth inning the thrashing was so bad that McGraw took out pitcher Clarkson because "his fielders needed some exercise" and installed Fay Thomas, a college student himself just a few weeks before. Initially Fay did well but fell in the ninth with "a slight attack of generosity with the result that the unfortunate situation developed of having the bases full with none of the school boys out."

The Buffalo Bison were beat in a hard-fought 6–5 game on March 10, but two days later the Giants were found on the downside of a 2–1 score to the Phillies.

Judge Landis (the *Sarasota Herald* called him the dictator) was making a tour of the towns of the Grapefruit League and arrived in Sarasota on March 14 to check out the team and the facility and get in a round of golf, he being "an old addict to the Scottish game," at the Whitfield Country Club, which was hosting a tournament between golfing greats Bobby Jones and Walter Hagen. The judge allowed he might stay an extra day and watch Jones and Hagen play. A former federal judge, Landis was a no-nonsense guy who acted on what he thought to be right and never wavered from his decision.

On the fourteenth of March the Giants took the Phillies 5–2 on nine hits with Tyson, Kelly and Jackson each hitting a home run. In the game with the Athletics a few days later they were even sharper, scoring ten runs on eighteen hits.

The day after, a large crowd at the Sarasota Kennel Club applauded heartily with Giants players as dog handlers led greyhounds to the starting line of the McGraw Cup race. The Washington Senators, the Giants' nemesis in the 1924 World Series, were in town for a three o'clock return match that promised to be the best game of the spring season. McGraw stated before the game that he was pleased with his team's progress, particularly the pitching department, which was much stronger than last year. He remarked that centerfielder Al Tyson, his acquisition from Louisville, was the most valuable addition to the club. George Kelly would start at first base, but, he said, "I know nothing of [Bill] Terry. He is a holdout." He went on, "I am pleased with my team as a whole." Underscoring McGraw's well-known eye for baseball talent, Tyson accounted for three runs in the Giants' 4–3 victory.

The Cleveland Indians, led by Tris Speaker, "invaded the peaceful settlement of Sarasota…with the war-like purpose of annexing scalps of certain spring citizens of this vicinity," but were soundly beaten 6–0. On the same day the paper announced that John J. McGraw had started building his residence near Golden Gate Point, indicating his intention to become a permanent resident.

The final spring game in Sarasota was on Friday afternoon, March 26, against Jack Dunn's Baltimore Orioles of the International League, which had several stars on the roster including $125,000 short stop Boley. The admission price of $1 was to be used to benefit the St. Martha's Catholic Church building fund. McGraw's men won 6–3. McQuillan sprained his left ankle tripping over second base garnering, Cross wrote, the spring trophy for hard luck injuries.

The next day the team boarded the bus to Tampa for a game with the Senators, and then on to New York, playing teams along the way. McGraw called spring training very successful and speculated that the season would be even better. "It is a very pleasing ball club," he said. "It is a better club than the Giants were last year, for the younger players like Jackson and Lindstrom have a year's good experience behind them. Tyson is a willing player and has strengthened the club. We are much stronger defensively with Kelly back at first. Pittsburgh is going to have no easy time holding the championship honors."

But the 1926 regular season would be a bust—one of McGraw's worst—the Giants managing only a fifth-place finish with 74 wins against 77 losses. One can speculate, as did at least one sports reporter, that perhaps McGraw was too tied up in the details of Pennant Park to give the Giants all the attention they required. (Interestingly, there was not one advertisement for Pennant Park, nor one report of its progress during the entire 1926 spring training season.) For his part, McGraw let it be known that he was not satisfied with how training went in Sarasota. He was quoted at the end of the regular season by *New York Times* reporter James R. Harrison: "Six weeks in one place is too monotonous. Besides it gets too hot in Sarasota near the end of March." He thought the hot weather was too much of a good thing; the athletes were baked out and over trained by the end of the training season. McGraw said that for 1927, spring training was going to be divided between Sarasota and St. Augustine, where it would be cooler at the end of March.

I don't like to sound egotistical, but every time I step up to the plate with a bat in my hands, I couldn't help but feel sorry for the pitcher.

—*Rogers Hornsby*

By spring training 1927, the conspicuous, full-page ads for Pennant Park, and most of the rest of Sarasota's inviting developments, had disappeared. So did the grandiose newspaper reports in the *Sarasota Times* and the *Sarasota Herald*. No mention of financial losses or editorials railing against McGraw for his failed development appeared in the press. It was as if the whole project had been swept away. In fact, an editorial in the *Herald* lauded John J. at the beginning of the training season as a baseball manager unequalled for year-in and year-out efficiency and told readers, "The glad hand of Sarasota is extended in today's *Herald* to John J. McGraw and his stalwart band of swatters."

[The only references to the demise of Pennant Park in the local papers I could find was a denial by John McGraw on March 31, 1927, that a surreptitious visit to New York was to sell some of his New York Giants stock "because he had gone heavily 'on the nut' in Florida real estate." In an article by Westbrook Pegler in the *Chicago Daily Tribune*, March 26, 1928, the writer said, "I have heard from retired real estate men in the Sarasota region that Mr. McGraw did something that not many other promoters of unsuccessful subdivisions did. He paid back as much as he could of the money that was attracted to Pennant Park." An item appeared in the *New York Times* of December 27, 1928, under the Securities At Auction section: "690 ½ shares McGraw-Pennant Park Corp. common; $5 lot." Next line: "217 shares McGraw-Pennant Park Corp. preferred; $5 lot." This was the ignoble close of a once grand plan.]

The Giants were quartered that year in the posh El Vernona Hotel, the Aristocrat of Beauty, which itself was beginning to feel the ill effects of the real estate crash.

A change in the attitude of townsfolk toward the players during their first season here in 1924, when the Klan felt duty-bound to march, to the players with the 1927 team is evident in a column by Floyd L. Bell, managing editor of the *Sarasota Herald*, who told his readers:

Sarasota has been chosen by the most colorful team in America as its training grounds, because of the climate, the sunshine and the general atmosphere of the place…It means that during the training camp season there are brought to Sarasota from 60 to 80 of the finest young men in the nation. There is no finer, cleaner, example of American manhood today than the average ball player. He is a gentleman, courteous, gracious and alert, keen minded and clear. It is a

Pictured here is the John Ringling Hotel; the New York Giants players, coaches and press stayed at this hotel in 1927 when it was known as the El Vernona Hotel. *Sarasota County History Center.*

distinct pleasure to meet and to be associated with these fellows...It means that the city takes its place at once on the map as one of the most delightful spots in America.

The paper reported that players, wives, managers and press would have the north portion of the hotel to themselves. The management was even going to provide the press with a typewriter lounge room where they would "find comfort as has never before been offered them." Among the press who covered the team were Richards Vidmer of the *New York Times*, Ren Rennie of the *New York Herald-Tribune*, W.M. Corum of the *Evening Journal*, Will Murphy of the *Daily News* and Frank Graham of *The Sun*.

The team that year acquired the services of star second baseman Rogers "the Rajah" Hornsby as a player/manager in a trade with Frank Frisch, with whom McGraw was always butting heads. Hornsby was one of the greatest hitters of all time (he was the National League batting champion from 1920 through 1925 and again in 1928). As player/manager of the 1926 St. Louis Cardinals he had guided that team to the world championship, their first in thirty-eight years. The Rajah signed a two-year contract with the Giants for $80,000, putting him just behind Babe Ruth in the salary department.

Also picked up in 1927, from the Cincinnati Reds, was journeyman fielder Ed Roush, a future Hall of Fame player who some conjectured at thirty-four might be too old to be a real help. The concern was unwarranted as Roush hit .304 that year and would live another sixty years.

Like McGraw, Hornsby lived for baseball—said he wouldn't read a newspaper or a book or go to the movies during the season because his eyes might be damaged. He remarked once, "People ask me what I do in winter when there's no baseball. I'll tell you what I do. I stare out the window and wait for spring." (The great Ruth shared Hornsby's fear of ruining his eyesight by reading. "Reading isn't good for a ballplayer. Not good for his eyes. If my eyes went bad even a little bit I couldn't hit home runs. So I gave up reading.")

And McGraw had no worry about Hornsby wasting time on the links. Hornsby: "I don't want to play golf. When I hit a ball I want someone else to chase it."

There was speculation that McGraw, whose men were said to be "automatons in his hands," and Hornsby, who had a mind of his own, might have a failure to communicate. McGraw fired players who didn't follow direction and Hornsby, "being naturally headstrong, and knowing that he is the outstanding star of the team," wasn't one to be ordered about on the diamond. The *Sarasota Herald* reminded readers that Hornsby had given both Branch Rickey, manager of the Cardinals, and also Cardinal owner Sam Breadon gray hairs because of his independent ways. Baseball historian Lee Allen said of him, "He was frank to the point of being cruel, and subtle as a belch." And Hornsby, like McGraw, didn't mince words. When Braves owner Judge Fuchs asked him whether he could win the pennant, Hornsby replied, "Not with these Humpty Dumpties." The *Herald* opined, "McGraw however, seldom makes fish of one and flesh of the other. Hornsby will have to take orders just like the rest of them although he is field captain. It will be interesting to observe just how the two 'Napoleons' get along."

Hornsby, with Roger Bresnahan, preceded McGraw to Sarasota and commented that the field looked to be in first-class condition. Under the supervision of Henry Fabian, "groundskeeper deluxe," an underground sprinkler system had been installed, the grass was bright green, the outfield smooth and the base lines of red Georgia clay were neatly laid out. Hornsby said the field looked like first division. "The boys are sure to be highly pleased with the changes made and the appearance of the park."

In a few days the *Sarasota Herald* noted Hornsby was the first one on and off the field during practice, unusual for a star of such magnitude. During batting practice he entertained the locals by "putting several balls in the distant swamp." It was conjectured that his diligent work was an attempt to win back the batting crown, and move up a notch in the salary department. The Rajah called it his "great opportunity," as success with the Giants would better his chances of taking over the team when McGraw retired.

The *Herald* also noted that Hornsby's "good natured direction" of the younger players would be but a pleasant memory in a few days when Little Napoleon came to town. It was felt among some of the coaches that with the acquisition of Hornsby, the Giants could place at least in the top three. The Rajah predicted that McGraw was due for another pennant that season.

McGraw was held in Havana by a storm but when he finally arrived and went to the ballpark to watch the action, Vidmer of the *New York Times* described his reception:

> *The Giants were going through their second workout of the day, and as it was hot and sultry and the morning practice had been long and strenuous there were very few signs of life. The pitchers were tossing the ball about. Roger Bresnahan was hitting flies up into the blue skies and panting young men jogged lazily after them…It was a listless scene. And then word got around that the stranger sitting in the shadows of the dugout was John McGraw and the name passed from one to another. The next moment every one began to hustle and bustle…The magic name of John McGraw turned the Giants training camp into sudden activity.*

Al Lopez, the great player/manager, had this to say about how a McGraw team practiced: "When they threw the ball around during infield practice, they really fired it; that's the way he wanted them to do it. When you watched that Giant team on the field, you could always feel McGraw's hand everywhere. He was all business on a ball field, and so were they."

Style differences notwithstanding, "Jolly Rogers" was expected to be a big help to McGraw during the spring training season, a person who could be relied on to actively coach and captain the team. The year's previous team captain, Frankie Frisch, had a passive style that displeased McGraw. "Frisch used to think his day's work was over when he handed the umpire the batting order. If I wanted to call his attention to something during the game, he generally was looking for his cap or a bird flying around or anything except the bench."

The 1927 season was Little Napoleon's silver jubilee as manager of the Giants, and while he looked his age he was still enthusiastic and full of vinegar. On March 12, 1927, the same night the team presented McGraw with a 4–3 win over bitter rivals the Washington Senators (a game in which his find, Mel

Now in Sarasota

ROGERS HORNSBY

Rogers Hornsby, formerly manager of the world champion St. Louis Cardinals and now playing second base for the New York Giants, who arrived with the advance squad of that organization in Sarasota Sunday and is daily working out here. Hornsby is probably the greatest ball player of the day.

A young Rogers Hornsby, one of the greatest sluggers of all time. *Sarasota Herald-Tribune.*

Ott, performed well), a testimonial dinner was given in his honor. The gala was held at the Venice Hotel and players, managers, coaches, league officials and newspaper reporters were all present. The whole lot of them journeyed to Venice in a caravan of cars, sounding their horns along the way.

(Later that year, in July, New York City honored its "adopted son" with a grand affair that included forty of Broadway's leading actors and actresses, a hundred chorus girls and such dignitaries as Mayor Jimmie Walker, Governor Alfred E. Smith and Commissioner Landis. Two bands gathered at Times Square and were taken by bus to the Polo Grounds. The fans would include five thousand disabled veterans, thousands of orphans and thousands of spectators. McGraw was presented with a large silver loving cup, topped with a silver statuette of him as he was when he broke into baseball with the Orioles. There followed a game between the Cubs and the Giants.)

Each training camp has its share of odd-ball happenings, but the accident of knuckle ball pitcher Fast Freddy Fitzsimmons was one for the books. Somehow Fitzsimmons rocked over his own fingers, putting himself out of commission. A

"Airtight Fred"

Fred Fitzsimmons, young Giant pitcher, who, with Mrs. Fitzsimmons, is with the Giant squad now quartered at the Hotel El Vernona. Official National league averages show that this young moundsman went through 37 games without an error. He accepted 62 assists and made 20 putouts.

Fred Fitzsimmons began his nineteen-year pitching career in 1925 with the Giants. *Sarasota Herald-Tribune.*

skeptical Vidmer recited the various ways players had tried to delay as long as possible the strenuous work of spring training: "Players, perfectly satisfied with the terms of their contracts, have held out valiantly in order to dodge Spring training. Some have delayed the grind by getting on the wrong train or missing the right one. Sore arms have been used for an excuse since the first fourteen stitches were taken in a horse hide, but this business of rocking on one's own fingers is new." Fitzsimmons was mute on the subject, probably embarrassed, and out of commission for quite awhile. McGraw "was so upset that he was on the verge of issuing an order denying rocking chairs to the players."

While big money was no longer being made in Florida real estate, 1927 saw an opportunity to score in black gold. The day after the Giants defeated the Senators, the *Sarasota Herald* headlined "Impressive Ceremony Marks Spudding In Of Oil Well." It is not known if any players bought or sold options, but for the grand occasion the ever-popular Hornsby was on hand to break a bottle of champagne on the drill bit and to hand out cigars to the men in the throng who came to watch the affair. (Unlike the short-lived but heady days of the land boom, no players held out from signing their contract with the hope of striking it rich in the oil business. Good thing, too—the only thing that ever gushed was smelly sulfur water.)

The Giants were scheduled to play seven games at the new and improved Payne Park: March 7, St. Louis Browns; March 8, Philadelphia Phillies; March 10, Buffalo Internationals; March 11 and 12, Washington Senators; March 14, Boston Braves; March 17, St. Louis Cardinals. After looking over the talent McGraw opined that "with good pitching, the Giants would stand an excellent chance for the National League pennant."

The final game of the spring season against the world champion Cardinals saw second basemen Frisch and Hornsby in the same game since their trade, and it promised to be a good show as each wanted to demonstrate to their former team manager that he made a mistake. The *Sarasota Herald* reminded its readers that only a few months before this game, Hornsby had taken the Cardinals to the World Series and was repaid by being traded away, unable to get along with the Cardinals owner Sam Breadon. Only McGraw had what Breadon wanted: Frisch with pitcher Jimmy Ring thrown in. Frisch had been popular with Sarasota fans, but so, too, was Hornsby.

The teams were not each other's favorites for another reason. McGraw had once said that "Manager Fletcher was doing a fine job with a bunch of sandlotters." The Cardinals' owner responded that unlike the Giants, his team was "not paying fancy prices for ready made stars."

On hand to perform before for the mighty struggle—the *Sarasota Herald* tagged it Greek met Greek—was the Czecho-Slovakian National Band. The "sandlotters" beat the "ready made stars" 3–0 thanks to a ninth-inning rally.

Prior to the game, McGraw had promised he would bring the team back for the 1928 spring training season and, hopefully, for several years thereafter. But for Sarasota and the New York Giants the game of March 17, 1927, would be the last hurrah.

During the regular season, the Giants managed a second-place finish, going 92–62. At season's end the big news was the trade of Rogers Hornsby, the hardworking second baseman and co-manager—"the strength and fighting inspiration of McGraw's 1927 team"—to the lowly Boston Braves who placed seventh, 60–94, in 1927.

There was much speculation in the national papers about the trade. Hornsby was certainly taken by surprise: "I can't believe it," he told a reporter. Neither could the public, who didn't buy Stoneham's "for the best interests of the club" story. Sports fans doubted that was the real reason. Both McGraw and Hornsby denied that it was due to a clash between them. Hornsby called McGraw the best manager in baseball. In a column in the *Chicago Tribune* titled "McGraw's Iron Hand Power Slips as Giants Head North," Westbrook Pegler wrote that club secretary Jim Tierney got Hornsby fired for telling him to go to hell. Pegler conjectured that the secretary, who owed his job to McGraw, had usurped some of Little Napoleon's authority.

It's a safe bet that the failure of Pennant Park prompted McGraw to look elsewhere for a spring training site. When he was hit on the ankle by an errant ball during a spring training game in 1928, preventing him from traveling to Ft. Myers with his team, Pegler, the nationally syndicated columnist, wrote on March 25: "McGraw had the misfortune or good fortune to be hit on one of his ankles by a batted ball…There are those who say this blow on the ankle was something in the nature of a favor to Mr. McGraw, because a trip through Florida would have awakened unhappy memories of an expanse of jungle near Sarasota which Mr. McGraw and some associates were retailing to investors of a couple of years ago at very interesting prices…If that blow on Mr. McGraw's ankle caused him a certain kind of pain, it undoubtedly spared him another kind. It kept him in Augusta."

1933–1958

It is going to be a long hard job, but we are going through to the end and eventually we will put the Red Sox back on their rightful heights.
—*Thomas A. Yawkey, Red Sox owner, 1933*

From 1929 until 1932, the fix for Sarasota's baseball habit had been supplied by the Indianapolis Indians, an American Association team brought to town by the chamber of commerce sports committee after having failed to persuade another Major League team to replace the Giants. But at the end of 1932 the Indians decided that because of the financial squeeze of the Great Depression they would be better off training in French Lick, Indiana, which was closer to their home. Once again the hunt was on for another team.

Enter the Boston Red Sox. If ever there was a team at the polar opposite of the mighty New York Giants, it was this era's Sox. A former powerhouse, they had placed no better than fifth since they won the World Series in 1918 and had finished last nine times through the 1932 season.

Managed by Shano Collins and Marty McManus, the team's 1932 performance was a disastrous 43–111, again good enough for eighth and last place. This poor season generated a scant 182,150 paid admissions into Fenway Park, which, in 1932, had a seating capacity of 35,000. By comparison, the first-place New York Yankees drew over 900,000 into the house that the traded Ruth built.

Immediately prior to spring training, 1933, the Sox had been sold by Bob Quinn to Thomas A. Yawkey of New York. A thirty-year-old heir to a $5 million fortune, Yawkey was a successful businessman who had a passion for baseball, which he got from his father who had once owned the Detroit Tigers. He was lauded in the press as a man of substance who had not let his money go to his head. (One story related that his mother had limited him to a dollar a week allowance, and once demonstrated to him his comparative wealth by putting piles of beans on a dish to represent the wealth of such as the Fords and the Rockefellers. On young Yawkey's plate, she placed one bean. He said the demonstration put his wealth in prospective.)

After he sold the club, Quinn apologized to the fans of Boston for not being able to put the Sox back on top. "I have been carrying for many years a load that would make most men jump out of a fourteenth-story building. I tried and spent plenty of money to build up the Red Sox. I failed and I apologize to the Boston public…I want to assure the Boston public that Mr. Yawkey and Mr. Collins are well equipped to build up the Red Sox."

The sale price of the once mighty Boston Red Sox was pegged at $1.2 million, and Yawkey promised an immediate rebuilding campaign to pull the Sox out of baseball's cellar. An Associated Press story recalled the Sox's quick dive into the status of perennial losers: Harry Frazee purchased the team from Joe Lannin in 1917 and ruined the club by selling off Babe Ruth, Everett Scott, Ernie Shore, Dutch Leonard, Joe Bush, Stuffy McInnis, Sad Sam Jones, Harry Hooper, Duffy Lewis, Herb Pennock, Joe Dugan, Waite Hoyt and some others. Frazee, a New York theatre man, was said to have made a fortune on the fire sale. The Sox took decades to fully recover.

At this time, Sarasota too, was striving to get back on its feet. McGraw had brought the Giants to a town on the move, boldly bragging that its growth could not be stopped as thousands of newcomers crowded in and property prices skyrocketed amid unprecedented construction. The real estate bust at the end of 1926, followed by the Great Depression was a one-two, knockout punch that put the county on its heels—a fate shared in 1933 with the rest of the nation. Taxes were difficult to collect, unemployment was high and public services were cut to the bone. Except for a few notable Works Progress Administration projects—the Municipal Auditorium, the Lido Casino, the Post Office—building in Sarasota practically ceased until after World War II.

Credit for getting the Sox to Sarasota was given to the baseball committee of the chamber of commerce, especially J. Paul Cobb, chairman; City Councilmen I.G. Archibald; and Walter C. Jungmeyer; and also to W.T. Simpson, secretary of the chamber.

The Tin Can Tourists of the World held their annual conventions just east of Payne Park from 1932 to 1938, drawing several thousand campers. *Sarasota County History Center.*

Another group was also lured to Sarasota. Mayor E.A. Smith invited the Tin Can Tourists of the World to change their winter convention site from Arcadia to an area around Payne Park, just east of the ball field. Much to the chagrin of the Payne family, a trailer park evolved—the Sarasota Mobile Home Park. It was not what the Paynes had in mind when they donated the land for "park purposes."

The first Red Sox players arrived with player/manager Martin J. "Marty" McManus and quickly went into double-session workouts. An AP photo of seven Sox players exercising with a medicine ball at Payne Park was given national distribution.

On March 9, 1933, owner Yawkey and general manager Eddie Collins arrived in Sarasota and for the first time since he bought the team, Yawkey was able to meet with his players. Collins said he liked what he had seen of the team during the workout and as he helped them prepare for their first spring game against the St. Louis Cardinals, indicated that he wouldn't wear a uniform: "I've had enough of that for the past twenty-seven years. I think I can forgo it." McManus said the club "had been strengthened over 40 percent by the acquisition of new players over the winter."

The Cardinals were practicing in Bradenton (Boston had trained there in 1932) and the game generated plenty of local interest because Rogers Hornsby, a favorite with Sarasota, was trying to get on the Cardinal roster as a second baseman, the spot still occupied by Frankie Frisch who had not yet reported. Hornsby was thirty-seven years old and nearing the end of a spectacular playing career. After the Giants traded him to the Boston Braves in 1928, he went to the Chicago Cubs (1929–1932) and was searching for yet another team.

The Sox won the game. In fact, they would beat the Cardinals twice during spring training in 1933, and Hornsby did make the team. He would play forty-six games with the Cardinals that year and then move on to finish the season with the St. Louis Browns.

Trying to begin what he hoped would be a winning tradition, McManus said he was going to play every game hard. "I'm out to win every ball game, exhibition or not." One of the stalwarts, Johnny Gooch, also reflected a change of attitude. He told sportswriter Jack Malaney that whereas "a quart a day used to be my usual portion," he hadn't taken a drink in over two years.

The pitching staff was praised by Gooch as one of the best he had seen in quite a while. Ace pitchers readying for the season were "Poison Ivy" Paul Andrews, Henry Johnson and "Junior" Bob Kline. Looking for a contract were newcomers Lefty Allen Jones, Mike Meola and Austin McLaughlin. Also trying for a spot on the mound was Walter Brown a right-hander from the Montreal club of the International League who was expected to add strength to the corps of pitchers. There was no talk of holdouts—this was the Depression and jobs of any kind were scarce.

Rounding out the team: catcher, Rick Ferrell; first base, Dale Alexander; second base, Johnny Hodapp; third base, Marty McManus; shortstop, Rabbit Warstler; fielders, Roy Johnson, Dusty Cooke and Smead Jolley. Also on hand was the well-traveled "Suitcase" Bob Seeds, looking for a place on the Sox roster.

The team managed to get through spring training without any injuries of consequence. On hand to help with first aid was trainer Moe Gottlieb, said to be the youngest man to hold a trainer's position with a Major League club. He had succeeded "Two Bits" Bill Bierhalter, who left after the 1932 season. Gottlieb had joined the club as a bat boy "after bumming his way south," and after a few years served as mascot and clubhouse boy, helping out the aging Bierhalter and learning the trade.

Press reports about Sarasota being sent to Boston were favorable, everything the chamber of commerce could hope for: "Sarasota has proved the best training camp the Sox have had in years."

The team had been put up in the Sarasota Terrace Hotel, an assignment they enjoyed, saying it was "a corker, the food was a revelation and to make it entirely perfect the Chamber of Commerce has kept away from the party and has not been around making promises they could not keep."

Payne Park, circa late 1930s. *Sarasota County History Center.*

In addition to the extracurricular activities that had entertained the Giants, Red Sox players could now fill their free time watching professional boxing matches at the American Legion Coliseum, less than a mile north of the hotel. The Bobby Jones Golf Course had opened in 1926 and there was no talk of preventing the players from golfing.

The field had been kept in good shape for them, and the right-field fence had been moved farther back. Someone had said it was so close that a "good hitter could bunt over it." (Gordon Higel, who had broadcast the Sox games in Sarasota, recalled that Babe Ruth didn't like the fact that the fence had been moved from 230 feet to over 300 between his visits.)

At the end of the 1933 spring training season the community showed its appreciation to the team by throwing them a dinner, attended by 120 fans of "the Bean City aggregation." Only Florida products were served, with fish being the main course. At the dinner Mayor E.A. Smith extended an invitation for the team to return and the *Sarasota Herald* editorialized, "It is the sincere wish of every fan in Sarasota that they will have the pleasure of listening in on the World Series in October and that our good friends, the Red Sox will be the representatives of the American League and return to Sarasota in 1934 as the world champions. But regardless of your position in the race, they will sincerely want you to come back here next year."

As Sarasota had been a late selection for spring training by former owner Quinn, only four games were scheduled at Payne Park. Not as many as the team wanted or, as it would turn out, needed, to prepare for the upcoming campaign. Games would be played on other fields in Florida and on the way back to Boston. The regular season opener included two games scheduled for April 12, 1933, against their arch-enemy Yankees at Yankee Stadium. The Sox would lose both games–the Curse of the Bambino still had many years to run.

For his part, Yawkey praised Sarasota, its fans and the park and promised that, indeed, the team would return in 1934. "This is my first trip to Florida and I am glad to be in Sarasota. Everything has been fine and the cooperation we have received while here and prior to the arrival of the team has been a marvelous thing. I look forward to a good many seasons here."

Thus began a twenty-five-year relationship between the Sox and Sarasota, a marriage between a town and a team that lasted until, as with some marriages, one unexpectedly walked out on the other.

The 1933 Boston Red Sox team improved over the 1932 version, managing to crawl out of the basement—just. Their 63–86 record was only good enough for seventh and drew to Fenway Park 268,715 fans, up from the 182,150 of the previous year.

This would be McManus' last year with the club; he would finish his fifteen-season career with the Boston Braves at second base. The 1934 Sox would be led to a .500 season by Bucky Harris who took them to fourth place with a 76–76 record, and brought the attendance numbers up to a more respectable 610,640. He would remain only one year, though, and the next in line to try to uplift the Sox was Joe "Mr. Clutch" Cronin.

> *A man has to have goals—for a day, for a lifetime—and that was mine, to have people say, "There goes Ted Williams, the greatest hitter who ever lived."*
> —*Ted Williams*

For the next several years, under the leadership of Cronin, the Sox and Sarasota fell into a comfortable relationship. Each March the Circus City welcomed the Beantown players, coaches, scribes and out-of-town fans, all ever-hopeful that—the "curse" notwithstanding—the Sox would turn it around.

Press reports back to Boston informed fans of the goings-on in Sarasota through Western Union sports operator Dave Rosen, who transmitted the thousands of words of visiting writers each day.

The clubhouse that greeted the Sox typified the Depression era—rundown and lacking many amenities. Joe Cronin was quoted: "Our clubhouse in Sarasota was a wooden building that was rat-infested. I think we had four showers in those days, and it was very small. Our training field itself was huge. You had to hit a ball at least 400 feet to get it out of the park, and in right field it was about 440." Money for facility improvements was in short supply in the struggling town, but to alleviate the effects of a strong breeze that blew in from Sarasota Bay toward the infield, a strand of quick-growing Australian pine trees were planted. (These trees would play a part in a 1960 game between the Yankees and the White Sox—Mickey Mantle hit a ball 410 feet to "a clump of trees extending over the wall, and it dropped into the playing field." Most everyone thought it was a home run except the umpire who said it was a triple and got into an argument with Casey Stengel over the call, which, naturally, stood.)

One of Boston's acquisitions was Mo Berg, one of the most interesting and colorful characters ever to put on a glove. Berg was a catcher who later coached but never distinguished himself with a bat. A linguist and Princeton graduate who was admitted to the New York bar, it was said he could speak eleven languages but couldn't hit in any of them. During World War II he was an American spy. Comedic baseball legend Casey Stengel called him the strangest man ever to play Major League baseball.

During the off-season, Yawkey had spent big money to acquire some major talent from the Philadelphia Athletics for the 1936 season, earning the team the name "Gold Sox." Among the big guns, he purchased the great slugger and first baseman Jimmy "Double X" Foxx, one of the greatest right-handed sluggers ever, who had batted .346 in 1935; Doc Cramer who hit .332 that year; and shortstop Eric McNair who had hit .270. The pitching staff was bolstered by the acquisition of Johnny "Footsie" Marcum, who went 17–12 with the Athletics. The new talent notwithstanding, the Sox managed only a 74–80, sixth-place, in 1936—a difficult position to swallow having spent so much money. NEA Service sportswriter Harry Grayson wrote that Yawkey's money did not buy a pennant and saw their situation as more muddled than ever by "juggling stars."

During the 1937 spring training season, Cronin was guarded about the team's chances. "We are not planning pennants this year. We are concentrating on winning as many games as we can. Where we'll finish, I have no idea."

Among the talent that year were young second baseman Bobby Doerr of the Pacific Coast League, third baseman Pinky Higgins, outfielder Roger Cramer and a pitching staff that included Lefty Grove, Wesley Ferrell, Fred Ostermueller, Jack Wilson and Johnny Marcum.

The emphasis was on rebuilding. Sportswriter George Kirksey warned, "Aging veterans with fancy salaries—including playing-manager Cronin—must hustle to hold their jobs. The lesson learned last season was costly but the effect has injected a badly needed hypodermic into a club that can't be as bad as its 1936 record."

Indeed 1937 would not be as bad, but the record was still a poor 80–72 for fifth place, twenty-one games behind the Yankees. But in 1938 and 1939 the Sox managed a respectable second place, again behind the always powerful Yankees.

Fateful 1939 was an important year for the Sox. Ted Williams—the Kid, the Splendid Splinter, the Thumper, Teddy Ballgame—was brought up from the Minneapolis Millers minor league team. Williams, a Sarasota favorite, began his nineteen-year career with the Sox with a first-year batting average of .327, which went to .344 in 1940, and a remarkable .406 in 1941. Like Rogers Hornsby, Williams made no bones about his hitting ability. It was said that when he first came aboard, his friend Bobby Doerr said to him, "Wait till you see Jimmy Foxx hit." The Kid supposedly shot back, "Wait till Foxx sees me hit." (Williams denied such a conversation ever took place but admitted the story typified his attitude.)

Later he was quoted, "If ever there was a man born to be a hitter it was me." Williams, who had made a name for himself with the San Diego Padres in the Pacific Coast League, was given the tag "the Kid" by the Sox clubhouse manager Johnny Orlando as soon as he walked in the clubhouse, late, for his first spring training in 1938. There he was, all of nineteen, lanky as a beanpole and, to put it mildly, irascible (some would say obnoxious)—a skinny kid with a quick mouth, who, then and forever more, did things his own way. He *lived* to play baseball, and was probably crestfallen when Joe Cronin, whom he called Sport, sent him packing with a few borrowed bucks in his pocket to the Minneapolis Millers team, training in Daytona. Characteristically, Willimas vowed he'd be back and show 'em. Before he left, he asked Doerr how much the three starting Sox outfielders made in salary, and promised that one day he would make more than all of them combined.

Playing by his own rules at all times did not endear Williams to many of the Boston fans or sportswriters, who, according to Williams were always prying into his personal life and seldom giving him a break. As he put it in *My Turn*

Ted Williams with J.M. Christie, one of the owners of Tucker's Sporting Goods. 'Tucker's Tackle Takes 'Em" was the store's motto. Williams was an avid fisherman. *Pete Esthus.*

A young Ted Williams with June deYoung Randell, 1939. *Pete Esthus.*

at Bat, "Oh, I really hated that Boston press. I've outlived the ones who were really vicious, who wrote some of the meanest, most slanderous things you can imagine. I can STILL remember the things they wrote, and they still make me mad."

As to his attitude he wrote, "Well, I had been a fresh kid. I did a lot of yakking, partly to hide a rather large inferiority complex. When somebody asked me a question, I answered it. Never very coy; never very diplomatic. As a result I would get myself in a wringer." He added about those early days, "But I'm still a kid, high strung and prone to tantrums."

Williams' signature song could have been Frank Sinatra's "I Did it My Way." He would not cater to *anyone*—fan or sportswriter. For instance, he refused to doff his hat to the fans as he circled the bases after a home run. Even at his very last at-bat in Fenway Park, after he hit a home run—what a way to leave the game—he still would not doff his hat to the cheering fans. It just was not in him to do it, he said. And he generally held sportswriters in contempt—which did not make for a sympathetic press—who responded by accentuating the negative elements of the Kid's personality while often failing to relate his positive traits, which were many.

Williams had to have liked Sarasota. For one thing, the press and the fans here were respectful to him and treated him and the rest of the Sox as guests and tried to make them all feel that Sarasota was their home away from home. Plus, Williams was a renowned fisherman, and in Sarasota in those days, the gulf and bay literally teemed with all manner of fish. Williams frequented Tucker's Sporting Goods Store, and when it was on Main Street he would go into the breezeway of the arcade and practice the art of fly-casting, at which he was expert.

Pre–World War II Sarasota was truly a sleepy town, especially if you were used to the action of a large city. Johnny Orlando recalled in Leigh Montville's book *Ted Williams, The Biography of an American Hero,* "Sarasota in 1938 was a hay shaker town. You could shoot a cannon up Main Street from Five Corners [Five Points] and maybe only hit a rattlesnake."

But the pace livened up markedly when the annual Sara de Sota pageant with its Grand Parade finale was held each March. The glamorous weeklong event drew tens of thousands of revelers to watch a beauty pageant, rodeo, coronation ball, boat races, dances and numerous other citywide events including everything from a children's parade to a frog-jumping contest on Main Street. The climactic Grand Parade was miles long, filled with marching bands and colorful floats with bathing beauties from around the state. Add to that the Ringling Brothers circus, also still in town in March, with its colorful performers, plus the simple delights of sunning, swimming and fishing, and the

A happy Ted Williams doing what he loved to do best. *Sarasota County History Center.*

sleepy town of Sarasota offered more recreational activities than many much larger cities.

Press coverage of the players in the local papers expanded to include features of their families in human-interest stories. Spring training was lasting longer and the players and their families were becoming more closely connected to the community, augmenting Sarasota's claim that more baseball players lived here than anywhere else. On January 6, 1938, *The Sporting News*, nicknamed "The Baseball Paper of the World," pictured six houses on its front page of a few of Sarasota's Major League players: Lloyd Waner of Pittsburgh; Lloyd Brown of Cleveland; Billy Sullivan of Cleveland; Paul Derringer of Cincinnati; Roy Spencer of Brooklyn; and Heinie Manush of Brooklyn. The feature was titled, "Their Places in the Sun—Where Big Leaguers Dwell in Sarasota, Fla." It was a far cry from the 1920s days when some Sarasotans felt invaded by young, hot-blooded ruffians.

> *I honestly feel that it would be best for the country to keep baseball going.*
> *—President Franklin D. Roosevelt to Kenesaw M. Landis, January 15, 1942 (The Green Light Letter)*

The Depression deepened, and in 1941 America entered World War II, and the fate of baseball was uncertain. Until Commissioner Landis got the green light from FDR, he was fully prepared to pull the plug on baseball for the duration of

The children's parade was part of the annual Sara de Sota pageant, which took place during the spring training season and drew tens of thousands to what was usually a quiet city. *Sarasota County History Center.*

This trailer park evolved around Payne Park. It was not what Calvin and Martha Payne had in mind when they deeded the city sixty acres of property for "park purposes." *Sarasota County History Center.*

World War II. But for the morale of the country, which had precious little to take its mind off of the Depression and now the war, the president opted to keep the national pastime going. Games were broadcast to the fighting men overseas who often formed their own teams for pick-up games wherever they were stationed.

Spring training, however, needed to be modified. No longer could the teams and their fans hop aboard trains heading for the warmth of the south or west. Railroads were especially vital to the war effort, carrying troops, armaments and supplies. Working with Joseph B. Eastman, director of the Office of Defense Transportation, Landis agreed to a boundary limiting teams to the area north of the Potomac and Ohio Rivers and east of the Mississippi River. This became known as the Landis-Eastman Line.

The Yankees ended up practicing in Asbury Park, New Jersey, and the Boston Red Sox at Tufts College in Medford, Massachusetts, then in Baltimore, Maryland, and in 1945 in Pleasantville, New Jersey. Exceptions were made for the Chicago White Sox, Cubs and the St. Louis Cardinals who could train in Missouri, Indiana or Illinois.

The players, of course, were not exempt from the war and many had gone off to serve. Ted Williams lost three valuable years to the service during World War II and would serve again during the Korean War as a Marine Corps fighter pilot. Baseball continued with the older players, those with deferments and "fill-ins" who normally wouldn't have been able to make a team. Even so, the games

Payne Park, spring home of the Boston Red Sox from 1933 to 1958. *Sarasota County History Center.*

Payne Park was also the home of the Sarasota County Sports Association softball team and the Sarasota Sailors baseball team. This picture, taken in Clearwater in 1947 shows the All Star squad team, which was defeated in the semi-finals. *Standing, left to right:* Jack Collins, Paul Eskew Jr., Orville Measel, J.L. Rowe, Joe Edwards, Cliston Taylor, Byron Jones, George 'Tiny' Johnson, Mark Wyatt (manager). *Kneeling, left to right:* Donald McGee, Skeets Gilford, Jiggs Joyner, Bobby Brown, Charlie Butler, Clayton Albritton, Buck Whitaker, Bobby Eslander (bat boy). *Not shown:* Bill Rutland, Pat Patterson, Reed Chadwick, Roland Metcalf. *Sarasota County History Center.*

offered a welcome balance to the war news that was particularly bleak for a long period after the Japanese attack on Pearl Harbor.

Sarasota became the home for thousands of servicemen who trained at the Sarasota Army Air Field. The soldiers there formed their own baseball league, the Payne Park Army League, called their team the Flying Tigers and took on teams from the surrounding area—the air base in Venice, Drew Field in Tampa, Camp Weatherford in Bradenton and Carlstrom Field in Arcadia. During the 1944 season the Tigers won fifteen games straight with their star pitcher, Sergeant Al Brabec, going 10–2 and their big-gun hitter Corporal Jim Daniel averaging .320. (The segregated black servicemen formed an "All-Colored" ball club, the Sarasota Colored Tigers.)

Sarasota High School also used Payne Park for their practices and home games. Sarasota historian Pete Esthus, a Sailor team member, recalled that

Pitcher Dave "Boo" Ferriss warms up at Payne Park, March 6, 1949. Ferriss, just out of the military, started with Boston in 1945 and went 21–10 his rookie year, followed in 1946 by a phenomenal 25–6. His career was cut short by a sore arm and asthma. *Sarasota Herald-Tribune.*

Above and opposite page: Welcoming the 1949 team. *Sarasota Herald-Tribune.*

since fertilizer could not be bought during the war, as it was needed in the manufacture of gunpowder, the infield was void of grass and some type of chalky substance called "Gumbo" was substituted.

When the Sox came back to Sarasota after the war, it was another sign of a "return to normalcy." The community had shared the angst of the rest of the country, and was now poised for another growth spurt, both in the number of returning snowbirds and also in the number of buildings and housing developments. Sarasota during the 1950s was less glitzy, less frenetic, than in the boom years, but its growth was surer and steadier. Folks bought property on which to build, not to resell as quickly as possible for a profit. For Payne Park, the growth included the addition of steel bleachers, which increased seating by twelve hundred in time for the 1951 season.

At nearly the same time, Sarasota benefited from its Circus City heritage when Hollywood came to town to film the Cecil B. DeMille blockbuster *The Greatest Show on Earth*. Some of Paramount Studio's major stars—Charlton Heston, Cornel Wilde, Betty Hutton, Gloria Grahame, Dorothy Lamour and Lyle Bettger—came to film and the community was truly star struck and in the national eye. The movie would go on to win the Academy Award for Best Picture and many locals had bit parts.

Another Hollywood hit from Sarasota was the movie *Fear Strikes Out*, which recounted Red Sox outfielder Jimmy Piersall's difficult battle with mental illness. Released in 1957, it starred Anthony Perkins as Piersall and Karl Malden as his father.

Dorothy Lamour, aka "the Bond Bombshell" for her work in selling millions of dollars worth of war bonds during World War II, was photographed throwing out the first pitch for spring training in 1954. Joe Cronin announced that she was going to be the West Coast scout for the Boston Red Sox. She quipped that if Bob Hope and Bing Crosby could do it, so could she.

Just as the 1954 spring season was getting underway, New York columnist Gayle Talbot wrote an article, "Are Training Camps Worth It?" According to Talbot, a lot of publications thought spring training was a racket and suggested that the same good could be gotten for the players from a few dunks in a Turkish steam bath. "As for the actual benefits, we've often wondered vaguely about that ourselves. The best conclusion is that it doesn't do any of them any harm unless they step in a hole on some minor league field, and that it undoubtedly does some of them a lot of good, especially those who are inclined to take on blubber during the winter."

The next day Ted Williams illustrated the downside of spring training. Having been in camp for only a few minutes, he went after a ball, stumbled and broke his collarbone. The injury had sportswriters prophesizing a dim future for the

The beautiful Dorothy Lamour showing 'em how it's done. She was signed by Boston to be a West Coast scout for the team and quipped if Bob Hope and Bing Crosby could do it, so could she. *Sarasota Herald-Tribune.*

Sox. Ben Olan of AP sports wrote, "the pennant stock of the Boston Red Sox, faced with the loss of Ted Williams has already slumped to almost microscopic proportions." For its part, the local press took the incident as an opportunity to cheer on the slugger, "We're For You Ted," wrote Phil Harris. "In his long and colorful career, Ted already has made more than his share of sacrifice. Twice he has answered the call for fighting men and served his country." As Williams was leaving for Miami, the *Sarasota Journal* ran a photo of him in his cast signing a baseball for a wheelchair-bound fan with the caption, "Ted Cheers Cripple." (That year the Sox finished fourth, going 69–85. Williams played in 117 games and hit .345.)

Newspaper cartoon showing the training locations of the Grapefruit League.

On March 2, 1957, Norman Rockwell painted a picture of the inside of the Payne Park clubhouse for the cover of *The Saturday Evening Post*. He portrayed an ungainly rookie holding a suitcase, bat and glove in an undersize suit. The legend to the painting was explained on the inside cover:

> *If Norman Rockwell, a Massachusetts painter, had allowed any diamond stars on his cover but the Boston Red Sox, he might have been ridden out of his state on a rail. So one day Sammy White, Frank Sullivan and Jackie Jensen, and Billy Goodman visited Rockwell, posed, and met his neighbors, which put him in solid with the neighbors...As Ted Williams couldn't come to pose, a stand-in played his position in top center; and that rookie is a local baseball whiz, Sherman Safford—but he doesn't go around looking THAT awful. Finally, at top left is John J. Anonymous. He once tried out for the Red Sox, waited years to be called and was overjoyed when Manager Rockwell put him on the team.*

In 1958 a silver anniversary party was thrown to honor this landmark year in the relationship between Sarasota and the Boston Red Sox. It was celebrated at the National Guard Armory with six hundred fans, a suitably large cake with lit candles and a gift of twenty-five golf balls from Wayne

Four members of the Boston Red Sox team. *Sarasota County History Center.*

Red Sox pitcher Tex Clevenger warms up in front of coach Del Baker in this 1954 photo. Clevenger stayed one year with Boston before moving on to Washington in 1956 and to the New York Yankees in 1961. *Sarasota County History Center.*

Spring Training in Sarasota, 1924–1960

Left and below: Boston players, suited up and ready to go. *Sarasota County History Center.*

Playing a game of pepper. *Sarasota County History Center.*

Ted Williams and friend leaning against a 1956 Ford Crown Victoria. *Sarasota County History Center.*

OFFICIAL PROGRAM AND SCORECARD—TEN CENTS

PAYNE PARK
SARASOTA, FLORIDA

WINTER HOME OF

BOSTON RED SOX

SPRING TRAINING GAMES 1957

GAMES AT SARASOTA

DETROIT	Saturday, March 9	1:30
WASHINGTON	Sunday, March 10	1:30
YANKEES	Monday, March 11	1:30
PITTSBURG	Wednesday, March 13	1:30
ST. LOUIS	Thursday, March 14	1:30
PHILADELPHIA	Sunday, March 17	1:30
CINCINNATI	Monday, March 18	1:30
WHITE SOX	Wednesday, March 20	1:30
WHITE SOX	Thursday, April 4	1:30
KANSAS CITY	Friday, April 5	1:30
PITTSBURGH	Saturday, April 6	1:30
YANKEES	Sunday, April 7	1:30

GAMES AWAY

PLAYED IN FLORIDA

Yankees at St. Petersburg	March 12	1:30
Brooklyn at Miami	March 15	1:30
Brooklyn at Miami	March 16	1:30
St. Louis at St. Petersburg	March 19	1:30
Yankees at St. Petersburg	April 2	1:30
Philadelphia at Clearwater	April 3	1:30
Pittsburgh at Fort Myers	April 8	1:30

The program for 1957. *Sarasota County History Center.*

Hibbs, president of the Sarasota County Chamber of Commerce, to Joe Cronin, then the Sox general manager. A beaming Mrs. Cronin was photographed holding a lovely bouquet.

In accepting the applause of the excited fans and community leaders, a broadly smiling Cronin shared his appreciation: "We have had twenty-five years of happy association with the people of Sarasota and have no intention of moving our training base to Arizona, California or anywhere else." The plan was to stay in Sarasota indefinitely. To underscore this happy announcement, Cronin read a telegram from owner Tom Yawkey, pledging to remain in the Circus City.

Before the evening was over, even Ted Williams, the usually reticent star, appeared on stage to show a film of him battling a 1,235-pound marlin. Spirits were high as the group filed out. Mayor Frank Hoersting was scheduled to throw out the first ball to open up the 1958 exhibition season against the Pittsburgh Pirates. Managed by Pinky Higgins, the 1958 spring season was one of the Sox's best showings. Casey Stengel rated them and Chicago as "the top threats to continued Yankee domination."

In May of 1958, as part of a $4.7 million bond issue for capital improvements to the city, $100,000 was included to give the ballpark a face-lift. Part of the money would be used to build a new clubhouse and the rest for lighting, improved seating and other upgrades. City Manager Ken Thompson replied "no comment" when asked if Payne Park would be as nice as the Braves' field in Bradenton, which had just undergone a major renovation. By comparison, a Boston sportswriter had said that Payne Park looked "Bush."

A bombshell hit Sarasota four months after the 1958 spring season ended. Caught unawares, Sarasota learned that their Boston Red Sox had abandoned them for Scottsdale, Arizona.

The *Sarasota Herald-Tribune* made the announcement with the banner headline of July 3, 1958: "RED SOX TO LEAVE SARASOTA." The afternoon's *Sarasota Journal* proclaimed, "Sarasota Stunned By Divorce." Comparing the news to an attack, the *Journal* reported, "Chief bombardier locally was the Bosox's number-one laughing boy and traveling secretary, genial Tom Dowd. But Dowd was all business yesterday as he scored a direct hit at City Manager Ken Thompson...Hit by the first pieces of shrapnel were Mayor Frank Hoersting [and the City Commissioners]."

A twenty-five-year relationship ended abruptly with an impersonal Sox press release:

> *The Boston Red Sox announce they will conduct spring training in Scottsdale, Ariz. for the 1959 season.*

> *The Los Angeles Dodgers will play a number of their exhibition games in Sarasota during the 1959 training season.*
>
> *These details will be worked out between representatives of the City of Sarasota and the Los Angeles club during the All-Star game period at Baltimore next week.*
>
> *Tom Dowd, Red Sox's traveling secretary, has been in Sarasota the last two days conferring with city officials and completing the agreement.*

The team's response was short on sentiment to the point of being terse—the community could have been forgiven if they thought they had been run hard and put away wet. Sarasotans' reactions were swift in the next day's *Journal*:

> Dave Boylston, the owner of Badger's Drugs: *"Frankly, I think it was a pretty raw deal to let us go ahead with this bond issue to get $100,000 to fix up Payne Park and on the spur of the moment to pull that kind of a trick."*
> City Commissioner John O. Binns: *"I'm just heart-sick over it and indignant at the same time. I think the association has been too long and too pleasant for each party for it to be broken up so suddenly."*
> City Athletic Director H.O. "Red" Ermisch: *"I think we got darn short notice. I feel the people of Sarasota are going to be very disappointed, especially in light of the fact they recently approved a $100,000 bond issue to make repairs."*
> Attorney Clarence McKaig, a season ticket holder: *"It's my opinion that they jumped the contract—morally if not legally."*

Other fans were optimistic that the Sox could be replaced without any difficulty. Tucker's Sporting Goods partner Bill Rutland said, "Sarasota is a town that's appealing enough so that in the future we won't have any trouble getting a good major league team here. The Red Sox are no great loss."

1959–1960

The Sox had been as much a part of the fabric of Sarasota's recreational life as the circus, the Sara de Sota Pageant, the Jungle Gardens and any number of popular attractions. They were *ours*—at least that was what we thought until we got bombed. (The *Journal* quipped, "[Sarasota] had found the beans in their part of Boston were Mexican jumping beans and they decided to jump from Sarasota to Scotsdale, Arizona. The BoSox also became the GoSox.")

With the loss of the Sox, the hunt was on again for another Major League team. On July 7, 1958, City Manager Ken Thompson, chamber of commerce sports committee chairman Willie Robarts (dubbed Sarasota's "Mister Baseball" for his efforts) and chamber of commerce manager Tod Swalm flew to Baltimore where the All Star Game was being played to pitch Sarasota to "one of the Big Sixteen."

The Dodgers had already expressed a willingness to train here during open dates even if Sarasota drew another team. During the city commission meeting of July 7, word was received from Ken Thompson that while there were no teams available for spring training in 1959, the Brooklyn Dodgers committed to playing at least nine games in Sarasota. The *Journal* quipped, "The Los Angeles Dodgers, those wonderful 'Bums' that formerly shot pool in Brooklyn, will play at least nine games at Sarasota's Payne Park this coming spring." Good news, and the hunt had just begun.

At the end of February 1959, some of the Dodgers' top brass were in town to finalize plans for a nine- or ten-game stint at the newly renovated and updated Payne Park, which included new locker rooms, a remodeled grandstand and an improved press box and concession stand.

A plan to welcome the team at the airport on Monday, March 2, and then drive them, parade-style, along Main Street and on to Payne Park fizzled because of a downpour that left over four inches of rain. The grand entrance parade was rescheduled for Saturday and the Dodgers remained in Vero Beach. The team would be introduced to the sporting locals and fêted at a chamber of commerce dinner set up by Willie Robarts at the New Terrace Hotel—formerly the Sarasota Terrace Hotel.

Three thousand fans showed up for the debut game against the Cincinnati Red Legs, which the Dodgers lost 7–2. Unfortunately for the Dodgers and many of the other teams in Florida's Grapefruit League, March of 1959 was unusually rainy. The Dodgers were rained out four times in Sarasota, a fact not lost on the Arizona press fanning the battle between the two states to attract teams.

According to the *Sarasota Journal* the Arizona papers were writing about "Florida Mud Ball." The *Gazette* in Arizona summed up Florida's weather problems: "Every team in the Grapefruit League yesterday was washed out once again. Checkers and parlor games played in hotel lobbies. No checker scores available."

Managers and team owners around the state echoed Bing Devine, general manager of the Cardinals, when he said, "Year in and year out, I'll take Florida over Arizona." *Sarasota Journal* sports editor Pat Putnam put the rain woes thus: "Yes we cry over the rain. When you have so many things to miss, who wouldn't cry? But when it rains in Arizona, it gives the population a chance to wash the dust off and let the blisters heal."

Attracting a team to come to Sarasota became—as always—a top priority for city leaders and the chamber of commerce, and their hard work quickly paid off.

Sarasota had negotiated with the Cleveland Indians, Baltimore Orioles, Los Angeles Dodgers, Boston Red Sox (forgiveness is divine), Chicago White Sox and the Cincinnati Reds, who were considered the favorite of this group because team owner Powel Crosley had been a longtime winter resident here.

Both the Reds and the White Sox had been training in Tampa, and it was decided that one of the clubs would have to leave. After consultation with Tampa Mayor Nick Nuccio, Chicago was chosen to leave and agreed to accept a pledge from Sarasota of $20,000 in advance ticket sales. In April 1959 it was announced: "Sox Switch to Sarasota."

A major problem arose that teams training in Arizona did not have to face. There, everyone on the team could stay at the same place. This was not true in the South. Jim Crow was still alive and kicking, and that presented a problem after Jackie Robinson broke into baseball with the Dodgers in 1947 and opened the door for other black players.

It was certainly a problem in Sarasota. (Not with the Red Sox, as they had not integrated during their spring training tenure in Sarasota.) The community was not on the cutting edge of segregation. John Schaub, president of the Sarasota Sports Committee and manager of Maas Brothers Department Store, recalled for an article in *SARASOTA Magazine* by Dave Barbulesco that one of the issues in attracting a team was providing quarters for the black players. Schaub recalled that when the Sarasota Motor Hotel was up for sale it was purchased with the intent to house the entire White Sox team there. That arrangement worked during the 1960 season but soon fell through. In 1961 the black players were put up in a motel on Highway 301. Schaub: "We moved in there when the White Sox came in 1961. Everything was set up…The Sox got here on March 20, and that night I got a call from the sheriff that there was a big problem out at the hotel. When I got out there, they were having sort of a block party. There were three crosses burning outside the hotel. It was kind of a rocky start but things got easier as we went along."

The racial situation was given attention in a *New York Times* article on February 19, 1961. An AP photo pictured a black couple sitting in their living room, Mr. and Mrs. K.W. Gibson, described as a "house mother" for the Negro members of the Milwaukee Braves. The Gibsons lived "in the Negro section of Bradenton, Fla.," and during the training season the black players of the team all lived in their two-story home.

The article ran down the list of towns that hosted Major League teams, and the only place in Florida where all members lodged together was Vero Beach, where the players stayed at an old air base known during the season as "Dodgertown." The players in other towns had to make arrangements with private homeowners or were put up in motels or boarding houses.

As for the Chicago White Sox in Sarasota that year, Bill Veeck, White Sox president, who had integrated the American League when he signed the great Larry Doby and, later, pitching ace Satchel Paige to the Cleveland Indians, began negotiating with town civic leaders to have "six Negro players, including Minnie Minoso and Al Smith, stay with the rest of the team at the Sarasota Terrace Hotel." He was certainly sympathetic to the plight of black players on his team. As the article summed up, though, "The Negro players probably will be put up at a motel."

Pitching ace Early Wynn, a three-hundred-game winner who was one tough hombre on the mound. *Sarasota County History Center.*

There are only two seasons—winter and baseball.
—Bill Veeck

The "GoGo" Chicago White Sox came to Sarasota in 1960 as the champions of the American League. (Thirty-five years earlier, the New York Giants had come to town as the National League champs.) Led by the great player-turned-manager Al Lopez, a Tampa native, and owned by a business syndicate headed by the irascible baseball showman Bill Veeck, the team was welcomed with a two-page spread in the local newspapers with a picture of each player, and the coach and manager above the retail business which "sponsored" him.

Veeck had long been a thorn in the side of baseball's old guard because of the showboating methods he used to fill stadium seats. He had grown up in baseball, his father having been an owner of the Chicago Cubs. Not only did Veeck turn teams around, his marketing stunts brought droves of fans to the ballpark. When he owned the 1948 Cleveland Indians they won the World Series and also set the Major League record for attendance—2,620,627—which lasted until the late 1960s.

Given his colorful personality and casual style—an affable guy, always in an open-collar sport shirt—he could not have found a more suitable place than laid-back Sarasota. His antics had gotten him dubbed the Barnum of baseball,

Chicago White Sox owner and showman Bill Veeck "the Barnum of baseball." *Sarasota County History Center.*

Veeck getting fanned. *Sarasota County History Center.*

and Sarasota, of course, was known around the world as the Circus City, home of the Ringling Bros. and Barnum & Bailey Circus. One of his first on-field photographs pictured him on a lounge chair being fanned with a palm frond by beauty Jo Ann Adkinson in a white bathing suit. On another occasion an elephant from Ringling Brothers was led out by Cheryl Christiani to present Veeck with a box of cigars.

His most controversial stunt occurred in 1951 when he owned the hapless St. Louis Browns (52–102). For one game, he suited up Eddie Gaedel, a midget, and sent him out to the plate. Eddie wasn't quite 3'7" and weighed only sixty-five pounds. He walked on four balls—all high. This bit underscored Veeck's style: "I try not to break the rules, but merely to test their elasticity," he once said. Another Veeck stunt was to have the fans in the stadium call all the plays—his team won the game. He also introduced the exploding scoreboard and various fan-appreciation nights to generate interest in coming out to the ball game.

Just as McGraw's 1924 New York Giants before them, the 1960 White Sox came to Sarasota loaded with talent. Future Hall of Fame inductees included manager Al Lopez, who had a nineteen-year career as a catcher followed by a fifteen-year stint as a manager of the Cleveland Indians and the Chicago White Sox, winning pennants in 1954 and 1959; pitcher Early Wynn, an intimidating hurler who once said, "I've got a right to knock down anybody holding a bat"; shortstop Luis Aparicio; and second baseman Nellie Fox. The team also boasted regular stalwarts like catcher Sherm Lollar; first baseman Roy Sievers, a power hitter picked up from Washington whose position he would sometimes share with big Ted Kluszewski who had been bothered by a bad back the year before; third baseman Gene Freese; and outfielders Minnie Minoso, Jim Landis and Al Smith.

Two well-known local boys were also on hand that year to try out for the team, former Sarasota High School standouts Roy Kirkland, shooting for a catcher's spot, and Billy Hicks, whom Lopez called a "fine prospect." Another local, Billy Goodman, was already well established having had an excellent eleven-year career with Boston before joining Chicago.

The 1960 spring training season had been extended to twenty-nine games with the Sox going 16–13, good enough for first place for the exhibition season with predictions that they would again be American League champs when the regular season ended. The spring season finale was a bittersweet game against

Autographing balls. That's not a hat above his head. *Sarasota County History Center.*

the Boston Red Sox that drew a large crowd of fans, many of whom had ambivalent feelings about their former team, having avidly followed the Red Sox in Sarasota for so long only to be walked out on.

According to the *Sarasota Journal*, though, most of the 3,081 fans at Payne Park that day seemed to be of the Boston variety. "Beantown fans were much in evidence as their applause drowned out the weak efforts of their Windy City counterparts. The 7th inning stretch proved their numbers." Sports editor Larry Howell said the fan ratio was evenly divided. "The White Sox no doubt sensed the 50–50 sentimental split in the enthusiastic crowd yesterday, but it should have been exhilarating. When they've trained 25 years in Sarasota, this is the kind of fan they will have gained."

Howell noted this post-game conversation between two fans:

> *"Boy, the old Red Sox still got it, haven't they?"*
> *"C'mon, Joe, the White Sox are our team now."*
> *"I know, I know, but until this year I didn't know there was another Major League team besides Boston."*

(Boston won the game 3–0. "Boston White-Washes White Sox in Season Final.")

Many rooters came out to see, perhaps for the last time, the Splendid Splinter, always a local favorite. He was forty-one years old, nursing many maladies, as the sport had taken its toll on his body over the years. In an interview by Phil Harris, Williams related that he was ten pounds overweight, had terrific neck pains and aches and pains all over. But that did not prevent him that day from belting one to the right-field wall, good for a stand-up double and also pounding out a solid single. (Indeed, Williams would end his career after the 1960 season. He played 113 games that year, hit twenty-nine home runs and batted .316, giving him a lifetime average of .344.)

Shortly before the 1960 spring season ended, a rumor began circulating that, improvements to Payne Park notwithstanding and in the face of a successful season, the White Sox might not come back. In terms of the numbers of fans attending the game, Payne Park drew far more than came out to watch them play in Tampa. In fact that year's Sox set the attendance record for Payne Park at 40,825. In his One Man's Opinion column, *Sarasota Journal* sports editor Larry Howell wrote, "Everywhere the White Sox go, they are asked:

All alone in the Chicago White Sox dressing room at Payne Park. *Sarasota County History Center.*

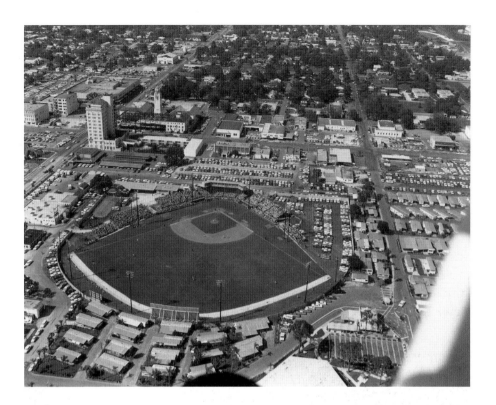

An aerial view of Sarasota's diamond.

'How're you drawing in Sarasota?' The Answer: 'Better than double what we drew in Tampa.'"

But still the rumors persisted, given credence, no doubt, by the community's sore spot after having been burned by the Red Sox. The notion was further fueled by the last game of the season between the Sox and the Sox. Conjecture had it that maybe the two teams were contemplating a switch in training bases.

White Sox vice-president and treasurer and former playing great Hank Greenberg quelled the rumors. "Everything's great here," he said. "Move? Just got here." An editorial in the *Sarasota Journal* lauded the quick response: "Obviously, we're happy to have the Chicago White Sox and gratified at the quick and puzzled retort to the rumors of any change in the five-year contract."

The White Sox's initial five-year commitment to Sarasota stretched to twenty-eight years, a time span during which they would be the last Major League team

Demolition of Payne Park.

to practice at Payne Park for spring training and the first to train at the new Ed Smith Stadium named to honor the hard-working, multi-year president of the Sarasota Sports Committee.

Located at 12th Street and Tuttle Avenue, it opened in time for spring training in 1989. The multi-million-dollar sports complex with its manicured fields, seating for nearly eight thousand and modern clubhouse is a far cry from old Payne Park. White Sox general manager Larry Himes was quoted just before it opened: "It's going to be the No.1 stadium in the Grapefruit League."

It will not be until 2055 that the Ed Smith Stadium will have stood as long as its venerable old predecessor. Maybe there will be a kid sitting in the stands with his grandfather on a sunny March afternoon, watching today's greats become tomorrow's immortals and he will be moved to write its history.

WHATEVER BECAME OF...?

Baseball is the only field of endeavor where a man can succeed three times out of ten and still be considered a good performer.

—*Ted Williams*

One of the greatest baseball managers of all time, JOHN J. MCGRAW, was born on April 7, 1873, and died of uremia on February 25, 1934. McGraw broke into the big leagues with the Orioles in 1891 as a third baseman, and during a sixteen-year stint as a star player hit .334. He managed the New York Giants for thirty years beginning in 1902, taking the team to ten pennants and three World Series victories. Although he had an abrasive personality he also had a kind heart and was respected by his players. The *New York Times* reported that thousands of people from all walks of life, from dignitaries to "bleacher fans," attended his funeral at St. Patrick's Cathedral in New York. He was eulogized as an inspiration to youth. Father Hammer told the congregation: "Our country loves its heroes and enshrines their names. No contemporary history of America would be complete which failed to record the contribution to America and to the progress and welfare of American youth by this sportsman and athlete of America." Thousands in the street doffed their hats as 110 honorary pallbearers marched beside his casket. Among those attending was Frankie Frisch.

FRANKIE FRISCH, "the Fordham Flash," who always had difficulty getting along with McGraw, was born on September 9, 1898, and died on March 12, 1973. Frisch broke into the big leagues in 1919 with the Giants and after he was traded for Rogers Hornsby in 1926 played for the Cardinals until 1937. During his nineteen seasons as a player he batted .316. From 1933 through 1951 Frisch also managed the Cardinals (with whom he won the World Series in 1934), the Pirates and the Cubs. He was inducted into the Hall of Fame as a player in 1947.

Bill Terry, "the Memphis Mauler" was born on October 30, 1898, and died on January 9, 1989. Terry had a stellar baseball career, playing first base for fourteen seasons with the Giants before succeeding John McGraw as manager in 1932. Terry had a lifetime batting average of .341 and once hit .401. Thereafter he autographed balls with his name and "401" below it. McGraw once said to him, "Bill Terry, you can ask for more money in winter and do less in summer than any ball player I know." For his part, Terry said of McGraw, "He was the type of fellow who would call all the pitches until you got in a spot, and then he'd leave you on your own." Terry managed the Giants from 1932 through 1941 with a career record of 823–661. He won the World Series in 1933 and the National League pennant in 1936 and 1937. He was inducted into the Hall of Fame as a player in 1954.

Rogers Hornsby was born on April 27, 1896, and died on January 5, 1963. One of the all-time great sluggers, Rajah won seven batting titles, six of them in a row, was two-time MVP and had a .358 lifetime batting average during his twenty-three-year playing career. As player/manager of the Cardinals he won the World Championship in 1926. Sportswriter John Kieran said of Hornsby, "So the record of Hornsby is that they admired him, they went after him, they got him, he did well—and they fired him, one after the other. As they say in baseball: That's one for the book."

Pitcher Alvin "Handsome Hugh" McQuillan was born on September 15, 1895, and died on August 26, 1947. Bought from the Boston Braves for $100,000 in 1922, McQuillan pitched for the Giants for six seasons, helping them win the league pennant three times in a row, 1922–1924. McQuillan went 11–10 in 1926 and 5–4 in 1927. During his ten years in the majors he compiled an ERA of 3.83. In 1929 and 1930 he played for the storied Toledo Mud Hens.

Pitcher Wayland Dean was born on June 20, 1902, and died on April 10, 1930. He pitched for the Giants in 1924, going 6–12, and 10–7 in 1925. He pitched for Philadelphia in 1926 and 1927 and retired with the Cubs in 1927 when arm problems ended his career. He died of TB at twenty-seven years of age.

Ernest Maun was born on February 3, 1901, and died on January 1, 1987. He pitched in the Major Leagues for only two years, for the Giants in 1924, going

1–1, and the Phillies in 1926, 1–4. His best year as a pitcher was with a minor league Wichita team in 1923 when he won twenty-six games.

Outfielder EMIL MEUSEL, "the California Cloutter," was born on June 9, 1893, and died on March 1, 1963. He played with the Giants from 1922 to 1926, retiring in 1927 with Brooklyn. He had a lifetime batting average of .343.

GEORGE KELLY had a sixteen-year career playing for the Giants, Pirates, Reds and Cubs, compiling a lifetime batting average of .297. He was once credited by John McGraw with making more important hits for him than any other player. He was inducted into the Hall of Fame in 1973.

FRANK WALKER was born on September 22, 1894, and died on September 16, 1974. He broke into the big leagues with the Detroit Tigers and played for three different teams. His last season was 1925 with the Giants. He had a lifetime batting average of .214.

WILLIAM PATRICK "MICKEY" DEVINE was born on May 9, 1892, and died on October 1, 1937. He played for three seasons with three different teams, breaking into the big leagues in 1918 with the Phillies, then in 1920 with the Red Sox and in 1925 with the Giants. He had a .226 batting average.

JACK SCOTT, the would-be real estate salesman and holdout pitcher, was born on April 18, 1892, and died on November 30, 1959. During his twelve-year career with five different teams he had an ERA of 3.85. His two best years with the Giants were 1925 and 1926 when he went 14–15 and 13–15, respectively.

One of the saddest cases in Major League baseball is JIMMY O'CONNELL, born on February 11, 1901, died on November 11, 1976. McGraw had heard of the minor league slugger and signed him to a record $70,000 in 1924. Pictures of the young Giant show a happy, handsome young man confident of his future. In 1925 he confessed to baseball commissioner Landis that he had offered a $500 bribe at the behest of his coach Cozy Dolan to Philadelphia Phillies shortstop Heinie Sand "to go easy on us" during the last game in the fight for the pennant. O'Connell also implicated Frisch, Kelly and Youngs, all who denied any involvement in the affair, were not disciplined and were ultimately elected to the Hall of Fame.

The much hoped for pardon from Landis never came. O'Connell later moved with his wife Esther to New Mexico where he played for a team in the outlaw Copper League. His games were piped into the TB ward at the army hospital at Fort Bayard, much to the joy of the patients. Later he got a job in California. Many thought the young man with so much promise had been the butt of a cruel joke. Landis reportedly said if he had only denied the charge, like the other three, it would have been a case of he said, he said and he would not have disciplined him.

FAY "SCOW" THOMAS was born on October 10, 1903, and died on August 12, 1990. He played only one year for the Giants, a total of only nine games, then went to the Indians and Dodgers. His Major League record was 9–20 with an ERA of 4.95. His best year as a pitcher was in the Pacific Coast League where he once won twenty-two straight games and had an ERA of 2.59.

JOHN WISNER was born on November 5, 1899, and died on December 15, 1981. He broke into the majors with Pittsburgh in 1919 as a pitcher and played for them for two years. In 1925 he joined the Giants and played for two more years, leaving in 1926, 2–2, with a career ERA of 3.21.

HEINIE SAND, the Phillies shortstop who it was said that Jimmy O'Connell tried to bribe, was born on July 3, 1897, and died on November 3, 1958. He played for six years, 1923–1928, all with the Phillies and had a lifetime batting average of .258.

ALBERT "TY" TYSON, John McGraw's big-gun centerfielder in the 1926 preseason defeat of the Senators, was born on June 1, 1892, and died on August 16, 1953. He broke into the big leagues when he was thirty-four and played only two years for McGraw, leaving after the 1927 season. He had batted .293 and .264 before leaving for the Brooklyn Robins where he played until July of 1928.

VIRGIL "ZEKE" BARNES, was born on March 5, 1897, and died on July 24, 1958. Barnes broke into the big leagues with the Giants in 1919 and during a nine-year career had an ERA of 3.66. In 1926 he went 8–13 but had a more respectable 14–11 in 1927. After going 3–3 in 1928 he went to the Boston Braves where he was 2–7 and later retired.

ED ROUSH, who had a sterling baseball career, was born May 8, 1893, and died on March 21, 1988, at the spring training ballpark in Bradenton, Florida, just before the Pittsburgh Pirates–Texas Rangers game. At ninety-four he had been the oldest living Hall of Famer. Roush had broken into baseball in 1913, and played most of his career with Cincinnati. Roush hit over .320 eleven years in a row. He played for the Giants for three seasons, 1927–1929.

ART NEHF, who came to spring training in 1925 and struggled to get his weight down, was born on July 31, 1892, and died on December 18, 1960. He went 11–9 during the '25 season and had a lifetime ERA of 3.20. In 1918, when he was with the Braves, Nehf pitched twenty scoreless innings but lost to the Pirates 2–0 in the twenty-first inning. His last year was 1929, with the Chicago Cubs.

WALTER "SLIM" McGREW, the tall player who did not come to terms with McGraw in 1925, was born on August 5, 1899, and died on August 21, 1967. McGrew had pitched three years, 1922–1924, for Washington where he played in only ten games and had an ERA of 6.60.

John McGraw's favorite, ROSS YOUNGS, who played outfield for the Giants for ten years, was born on April 10, 1897, and died on October 22, 1927. When he traveled with the 1926 team a nurse accompanied him as he had Bright's disease. During his career he had a .322 batting average and was inducted into the Hall of Fame in 1972.

"LAUGHING LARRY" DOYLE, the second baseman who felt great at being young and a Giant, broke into the big leagues in 1907. He was born on July 31, 1886, and died on March 1, 1974. During his fourteen seasons, mostly with the Giants, he batted .290 and retired after the 1920 season.

Pitcher FRED FITZSIMMONS, aka "Fitz" or "Fat Freddie," started with the Giants in 1925 and played thirteen seasons before switching to the Brooklyn Dodgers in the last half of the 1937 season. Fitz had excellent control and preferred to throw the knuckleball. He had a winning percentage of nearly .600 and a nineteen-year career ERA of 3.51. After he quit pitching, Fitzsimmons managed the Philadelphia Phillies from 1943 to 1945, coached for several teams and ended his career in 1960. Born on July 28, 1901, Fitz died on November 18, 1979.

THOMAS YAWKEY, who owned the Boston Red Sox for forty-seven years, was born on February 21, 1903, and died on July 9, 1976. Yawkey began the charitable Yawkey Foundation to fund the Tom Yawkey Wildlife Center. The foundation also contributes to numerous other charitable organizations. He was named to the Hall of Fame in 1980.

Spring Training in Sarasota, 1924–1960

John Shano Collins, a member of the "famous $100,000 infield" of Connie Mack's Philadelphia Athletics, batted .333, was a great base stealer and played in six World Series games. His managing career with Boston was less successful. During a two-year stint, 1931–1932, he managed only 73 wins against 134 losses. Born on December 4, 1885, Collins died on September 10, 1955.

Born in Chicago on March 14, 1900, Martin "Marty" McManus, a great infielder, began his fifteen-year playing career with the St. Louis Browns in 1920. In 1926 he began a five-year stint with the Detroit Tigers, went to the Boston Red Sox for three years and spent his last year with the Boston Braves. As player/manager with Boston in 1932 and 1933 he posted a 95–153 win/loss record for an average of 383 percent. During his playing career, he had a lifetime batting average of .289. He died on February 18, 1966.

Joe Cronin was born on October 12, 1906, and died on September 7, 1984. He began his playing career with the Pittsburgh Pirates in 1926. He then played seven seasons with the Washington Senators (1928–1934) and went to the Boston Red Sox in 1935 until 1945. During a twenty-season playing career he batted .301. His managerial record with Washington and Boston was .540, with a won-loss record of 1,236–1,055. He was inducted into the Hall of Fame in 1956.

Ted Williams was born on August 30, 1918, and died in Inverness, Florida, on July 5, 2002. The mighty slugger who wanted to be known as the greatest hitter of all time played nineteen seasons with the Red Sox, compiling a lifetime batting average of .344. He hit .400 or better three times. One of his fellow players said of him, "He could hit better with a broken arm than we could with two good arms." Williams was inducted into the Hall of Fame in 1966.

Billy Goodman was born on March 22, 1926, and died in Sarasota on October 1, 1984. A versatile player, Goodman began his sixteen-season career with Boston in 1947, played briefly with Baltimore before going to the White Sox and played his last year with the Astros in 1962. Goodman had a lifetime batting average of .300 and led the American League in batting in 1950 with a .354 average. A longtime Sarasota resident, Goodman was a World War II veteran of the navy and received the Citizen of the Year award from the Sunrise Kiwanis Club.

Jimmy Piersall, whose battle with mental illness was the basis of his book and the 1957 film *Fear Strikes Out*, was born November 14, 1929, and began his seventeen-year Major League career with Boston in 1950 as an outfielder/shortstop. Piersall was quite a colorful character. When he hit his hundredth home run with the Mets, he ran the bases backward. After his baseball career he became a sports announcer. Piersall had a lifetime batting average of .272, won the Gold Glove in 1959 and 1960 and was an All Star in 1954 and 1956.

One of the three DiMaggio brothers to play in the majors, DOM DiMAGGIO, "The Little Professor," played all of his eleven seasons with the Boston Red Sox. An All Star seven times, DiMaggio was a gifted fielder with a batting average of .298. In 1949 he hit in thirty-four straight games.

BILL VEECK, the showman-club-owner tagged "the Barnum of baseball," was born on February 9, 1914, and died on January 2, 1986. Veeck once said, "The most beautiful thing in the world is a ball park filled with people," and he was known for his willingness to do practically anything to bring the fans into the stadium. Veeck's father was president of the Chicago Cubs and Veeck started out in the concession business as a young boy.

He would go on to own three teams: the Cleveland Indians, who won the World Series in 1948, the St. Louis Cardinals and the Chicago White Sox, who won the American League pennant in 1959. Veeck, who was a champion of the civil rights movement, hired the first black player in the American League, Larry Doby, and the oldest rookie, forty-two-year-old Satchel Paige.

Veeck lost his foot serving with the marines in the South Pacific during World War II. (His leg was later amputated.) Inducted into the Hall of Fame in 1991, he is remembered on his plaque as "A champion of the little guy."

NELLIE FOX was born on Christmas Day 1927 and died December 1, 1975. One of the key ingredients to the success of the GoGo Sox, Fox was a twelve-time All Star who never struck out more than eighteen times in a season, going one year ninety-eight games without a strikeout. The 1959 MVP second baseman, with the ever-present plug of tobacco bulging in his cheek, played nineteen seasons and compiled a lifetime batting average of .288. He was elected to the Hall of Fame in 1997. The great Yankee pitcher Whitey Ford said of Fox, "Nellie was the toughest out for me. In twelve years I struck him out once and I think the umpire blew the call." And of Fox's personality, Ted Williams was quoted, "I just loved him. As a person, as an individual, you couldn't possibly not love him."

LUIS APARICIO was born in Maracaibo, Venezuela, on April 29, 1934, and took over the position of shortstop on the Chicago White Sox from another

Venezuelan, Chico Carrasquel. American League rookie of the year and another key to the GoGo Sox success, Aparacio had an eighteen-season career, led the American League in fielding for eight years and led the league in stolen bases his first nine seasons. "Little Louie," an All Star ten times, was inducted into the Hall of Fame in 1984.

Al Lopez was born in Tampa on August 20, 1908. After a nineteen-year career as a catcher, he managed the Cleveland Indians from 1951 through 1956 and the Chicago White Sox from 1957 through 1965 and 1968 to 1969, compiling a winning average of .581 and winning two pennants. Of managing a baseball team he said, "Managing can be more discouraging than playing, especially when you're losing, because when you're a player there are at least individual goals you can shoot for. When you're the manager all the worries of the team become your worries." He was inducted into the Hall of Fame in 1977. Lopez died in Tampa on October 30, 2005.

Local favorite Early Wynn was born on January 6, 1920, and died in Venice, Florida, on April 4, 1999. He began his twenty-three-year pitching career with the Senators in 1939, then played for the Indians, the White Sox and threw his 300th win for Cleveland. An intimidating fastball thrower, Wynn won the Cy Young Award in 1959 at age thirty-nine by winning twenty-two games. He won twenty or more games five times. His hard-nosed pitching philosophy was summed up this way: "I've got a right to knock down anybody holding a bat." He was inducted into the Hall of Fame in 1972.

Gary Peters was born on April 21, 1937, and still resides in Sarasota. The Chicago White Sox and Boston Red Sox ace pitcher was American League rookie of the year in 1963, going 19–8. He led the league in ERAs in 1963 and 1966 and was an All Star in 1964 and 1967. In 1964 he led the league in wins. He compiled a career record of 124–103, and ended his fourteen-year career in 1972 with Boston.

BIBLIOGRAPHY

Barbulesco, Dave. "Baseball Stories," *SARASOTA Magazine*, March 1994.

BaseballLibrary.com

Baseball-Reference.com

The Baseballpage.com

Burke, Larry. *Baseball Chronicles, A Decade-by-Decade History of the All-American Pastime*. New York: Michael Friedman Publishing Group, Inc., 1995.

Honig, Donald. *The National League, an Illustrated History*. New York: Crown Publishers, Inc., 1983.

Nemec, David, and Peter Palmer. *1001 Fascinating Baseball Facts*. Stamford, CT: Longmeadow Press, 1993.

The News

New York Times. Various issues from February and March 1924 through 1932.

Ritter, Lawrence, and Donald Honig. *The Image of Their Greatness, An Illustrated History of Baseball from 1900 to the Present*. New York: Crown Publishers, Inc., 1979.

The Sarasota County Times

Sarasota Herald

Sarasota Herald-Tribune

The Sarasota Journal

Wallace, Joseph, ed. *The Baseball Anthology, 125 Years of Stories, Poems, Articles, Photographs, Drawings, Interviews, Cartoons, and Other Memorabilia*. New York: Harry N. Abrams, Inc., 1994.

Williams, Ted. *My Turn at Bat, The Story of My Life*. As told to John Underwood. New York: Simon and Schuster, 1969.